Anonymous

Emory Hymnal

a collection of sacred hymns and music for use in public worship, Sunday schools, social meetings and family worship

Anonymous

Emory Hymnal
a collection of sacred hymns and music for use in public worship, Sunday schools, social meetings and family worship

ISBN/EAN: 9783337286262

Printed in Europe, USA, Canada, Australia, Japan

Cover: Foto ©Lupo / pixelio.de

More available books at **www.hansebooks.com**

THE EMORY HYMNAL

A COLLECTION OF

SACRED HYMNS AND MUSIC

FOR USE IN

PUBLIC WORSHIP, SUNDAY-SCHOOLS, SOCIAL MEETINGS AND FAMILY WORSHIP.

COMMITTEE ON SELECTIONS:

REV. L. T. WIDERMAN,
REV. ANDREW LONGACRE,
REV. GEORGE W. SHRECK,
WILLIAM RUDOLPH,
J. FRANK SUPPLEE,
WM. C. JENNESS,

CHAS. J. TAYLOR,
JOHN T. GRAPE,
JOSEPH F. HINDES,
SAM'L J. HINDES,
ED. A. HARTMAN,
GEORGE HASLUP,

ROBT. HASLUP,
HARRY SANDERS,
BENSON M. GREENE,
S. FRANK BENNETT,
THEO. WILCOX.

PHILADELPHIA:
JOHN J. HOOD,
1018 Arch Street.

BALTIMORE:
Grape, Taylor & Supplee,
203 Camden Street.

Copyright, 1887, by John J. Hood.

PREFACE.

REALIZING the need of a collection of hymns for use by the Emory Grove camp meetings, a committee of musical directors from the churches of the varied branches of Methodism in Baltimore was selected to compile such a work.

The need of a collection of hymns and tunes for all the varied forms of divine service soon became apparent, and the purposes and scope of the undertaking were accordingly enlarged. The aim of the committee has been to glean from all fields the choicest flowers of sacred song, and to present to the church a bouquet of hymns alike grateful to congregation and school, prayer meeting and the social circle.

There has been just criticism upon the poor poetry and worse theology of some of the hymns sung in our churches. To correct this evil, a judicious committee of Divines has carefully examined almost every verse, and has resolutely rejected all which are of inferior quality or doubtful meaning.

There has also been a careful revision and inspection of the tunes used, in order especially that melodies as thin as air shall not be married to words expressing the deepest phases of religious fervor.

The committee return their grateful acknowledgments to the many kind friends who have so generously assisted them by free use of valuable copyrights, by unstinted donation of new selections, and much helpful advice and assistance.

May the Master of Assemblies, before whom the majestic choir of the redeemed hosts praise night and day, make this work a blessing to all who use it is the fervent prayer of

THE COMMITTEE.

EMORY HYMNAL.

1. Our Glad Jubilee.

W. F. S.   "Thou crownest the year with thy goodness."—Ps. lxv. 11.   WM. F. SHERWIN.

1. Wake, wake the song! our glad jubilee Once more we hail with sweet melody,
2. Marching to Zion, dear, blessed home! Lord, by thy mercy hither we come;
3. Yet once again the anthem repeat, Join ev'ry voice the Master to greet;

D. C.—Wake, wake the song, etc.

Bring-ing our hymns of praise un-to thee, O most ho-ly Lord!
Guide us, we pray, wher-e'er we may roam, Keep us in thy fear;
Love's sac-ri-fice we lay at his feet, In his tem-ple now;

Praise for thy care by day and by night, Praise for the homes by love made so bright;
Fill ev-'ry soul with love all divine, Now cause thy face upon us to shine;
Jesus, accept the off'ring we bring, Blending with songs the odors of spring;

Thanks for the pure and soul-cheering light Beaming from thy word. Then
Grant that our hearts may truly be thine All the com-ing year.
Still of thy wondrous love we will sing, Till in heaven we bow.

By permission.

Take me as I am.

Copyright, 1878, by John J. Hood.

CHARLOTTE ELLIOTT.   **JUST AS I AM.**   Tune and Chorus above.

1 JUST as I am, without one plea,
But that thy blood was shed for me,
And that thou bid'st me come to thee,
   O Lamb of God, I come!

2 Just as I am, and waiting not
To rid my soul of one dark blot,
To thee whose blood can cleanse each
   O Lamb of God, I come! [spot,

3 Just as I am, though tossed about
With many a conflict, many a doubt,
Fightings within, and fears without,
   O Lamb of God, I come!

4 Just as I am—poor, wretched, blind;
Sight, riches, healing of the mind,
Yea, all I need, in thee to find,
   O Lamb of God, I come!

5 Just as I am—thou wilt receive,
Wilt welcome, pardon, cleanse, relieve;
Because thy promise I believe,
   O Lamb of God, I come!

6 Just as I am—thy love unknown
Hath broken every barrier down,
Now, to be thine, yea, thine alone,
   O Lamb of God, I come!

Jesus will give you Rest.

FANNY J. CROSBY.   JNO. R. SWENEY.

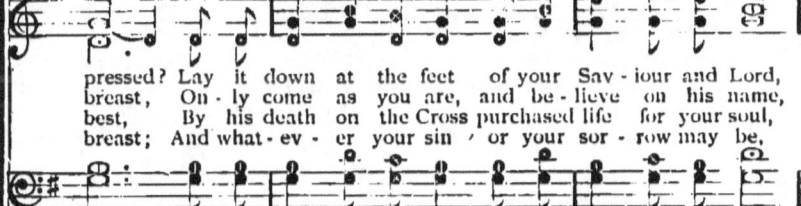

1. Will you come, will you come, with your poor broken heart, Burden'd and sin-op-
2. Will you come, will you come? there is mercy for you, Balm for your ach- ing
3. Will you come, will you come, you have nothing to pay; Je-sus, who loves you
4. Will you come, will you come? how he pleads with you now! Fly to his lov- ing

pressed? Lay it down at the feet of your Sav-iour and Lord,
breast, On- ly come as you are, and be-lieve on his name,
best, By his death on the Cross purchased life for your soul,
breast; And what-ev- er your sin or your sor- row may be,

REFRAIN.

Je- sus will give you rest. Oh, hap-py rest! sweet, happy rest!

Je- sus will give you rest, Oh! why won't you come in

.happy rest,

sim- ple, trust- ing faith? Je- sus will give you rest.

From "Joy to the World," by per.

DO RE MI FA SO LA MI

Hopefully Trusting.

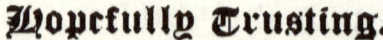

CALLENA FISK. "Peace through the blood of his cross."—Col. i. 20. JOHN T. GRAPE. By per.

1. I stand all be-wil-dered with won-der, And gaze on the o-cean of love, And o-ver its waves to my spir-it Comes peace, like a heav-en-ly dove.

2. I strug-gled and wres-tled to win it,— The bless-ing that set-teth me free,— But when I had ceased from my strug-gles, His peace Je-sus gave un-to me.

3. He laid his hand on me and healed me, And bade me be ev-'ry whit whole; I touched but the hem of his gar-ment, And glo-ry came thrill-ing my soul.

4. The Prince of my Peace is now pass-ing, The light of his face is on me; But lis-ten, be-lov-ed, he speak-eth, "My peace will I give un-to thee."

D.S.—In Je-sus I'm hopeful-ly trust-ing, My will is the will of my God.

CHORUS.

The cross now covers my sins, The past is un-der the blood,

Sound the Battle Cry.

W. F. S.
WM. F. SHERWIN. By per.

Vigorously, in march time.

1. Sound the bat-tle cry, See! the foe is nigh; Raise the standard high For the Lord; Gird your ar-mor on, Stand firm ev-'ry one, Rest your cause up-on his ho-ly word.
2. Strong to meet the foe, March-ing on we go, While our cause we know Must pre-vail; Shield and ban-ner bright, Gleam-ing in the light, Bat-tling for the right, we ne'er can fail.
3. Oh! thou God of all, Hear us when we call, Help us, one and all, By thy grace; When the bat-tle's done, And the vic-t'ry won, May we wear the crown be-fore thy face.

CHORUS.

Rouse, then, sol-diers! ral-ly round the banner! Ready, stead-y, pass the word a-long; Onward, forward, shout a-loud, Ho-san-na! Christ is Captain of the migh-ty throng.

2d CHO.—*Rouse, then, freemen, come from hill and valley; Fathers, brothers, earnest, brave, and strong! Onward, forward, all u-nit-ed ral-ly, "Death to Alchohol!" your bat-tle song.*

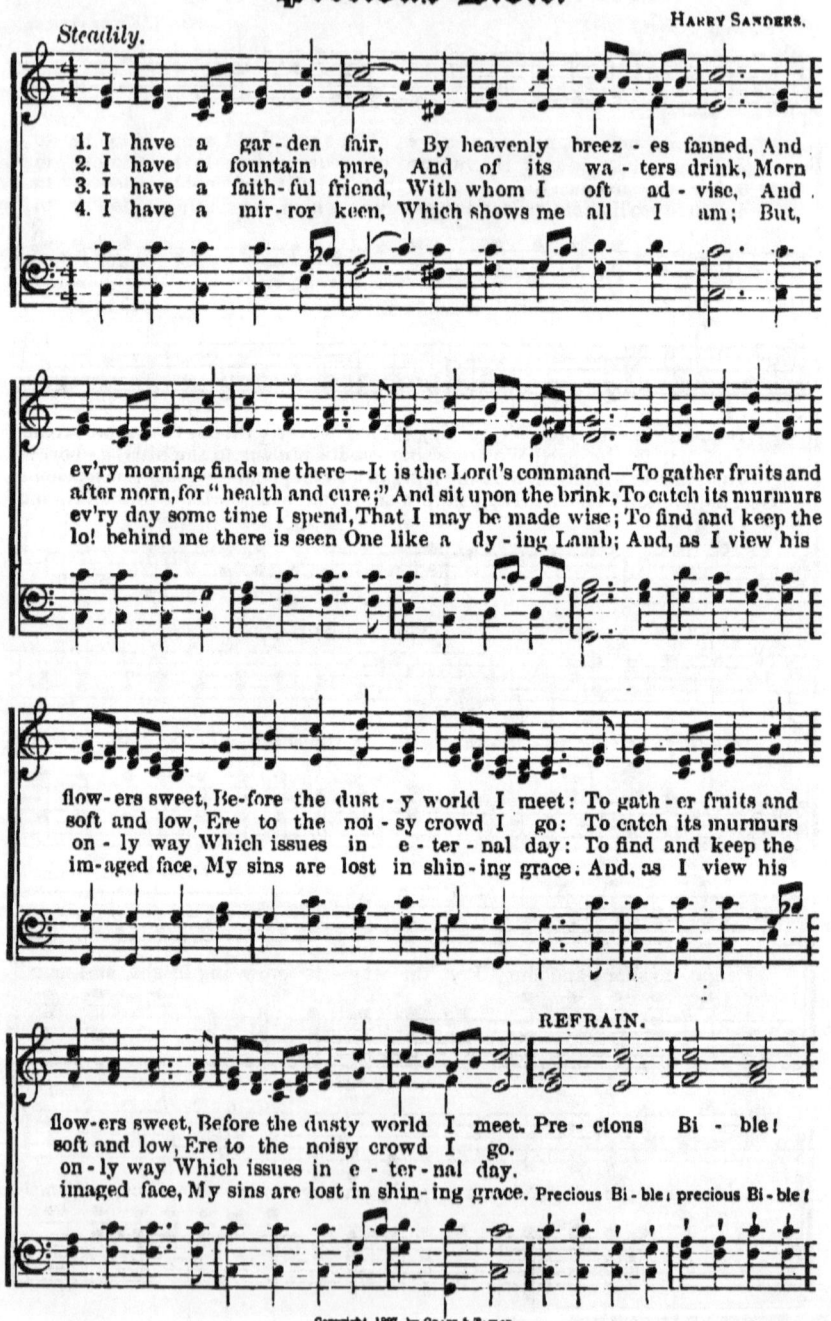

28. Tell it to Jesus.

J. E. RANKIN, D.D.   Matt. xiv. 12.   E. S. LORENZ.

1. Are you wea-ry, are you heavy-heart-ed? Tell it to Je-sus,
2. Do the tears flow down your cheeks unbidden? Tell it to Je-sus,
3. Do you fear the gath'ring clouds of sor-row? Tell it to Je-sus,
4. Are you trou-bled at the thought of dy-ing? Tell it to Je-sus,

Tell it to Je-sus; Are you griev-ing o-ver joys de-part-ed?
Tell it to Je-sus; Have you sins that to man's eye are hid-den?
Tell it to Je-sus; Are you anx-ious what shall be to-mor-row?
Tell it to Je-sus; For Christ's coming Kingdom are you sigh-ing?

CHORUS.

Tell it to Je-sus a-lone. Tell it to Je-sus, Tell it to Je-sus, He is a friend that's well known; You have no oth-er such a friend or broth-er, Tell it to Je-sus a-lone.

By permission.

30. Rejoicing Evermore.

JOHN NEWTON.   R. E. HUDSON.

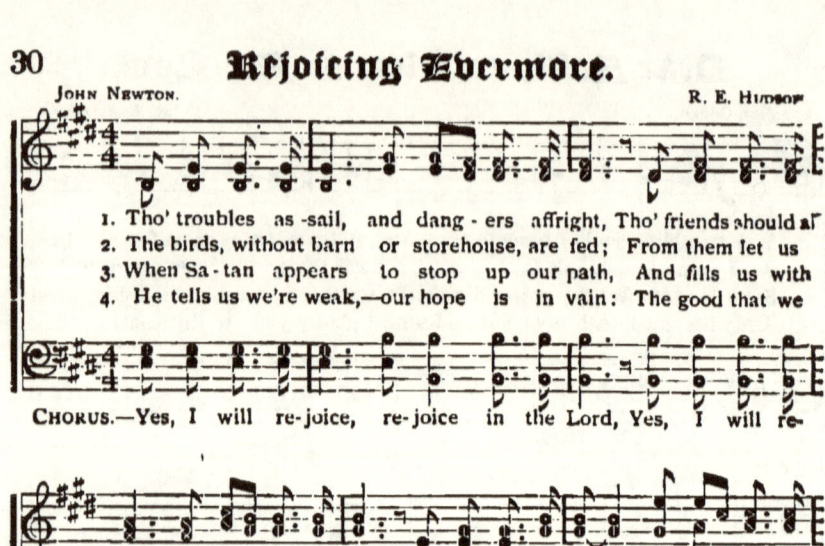

1. Tho' troubles as-sail, and dang-ers affright, Tho' friends should all
2. The birds, without barn or storehouse, are fed; From them let us
3. When Sa-tan appears to stop up our path, And fills us with
4. He tells us we're weak,—our hope is in vain: The good that we

CHORUS.—Yes, I will re-joice, re-joice in the Lord, Yes, I will re-

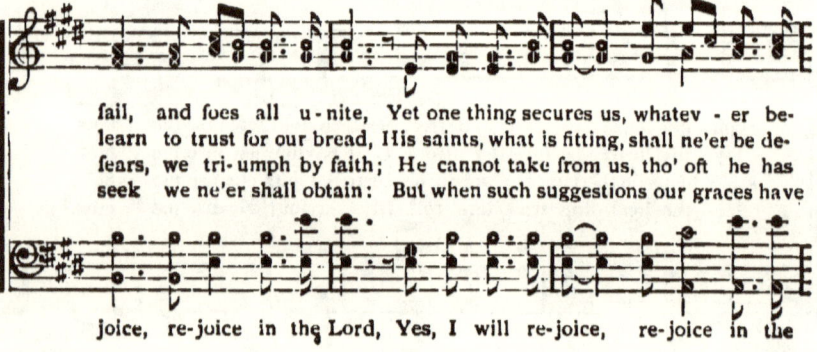

fail, and foes all u-nite, Yet one thing secures us, whatev-er be-
learn to trust for our bread, His saints, what is fitting, shall ne'er be de-
fears, we tri-umph by faith; He cannot take from us, tho' oft he has
seek we ne'er shall obtain: But when such suggestions our graces have

joice, re-joice in the Lord, Yes, I will re-joice, re-joice in the

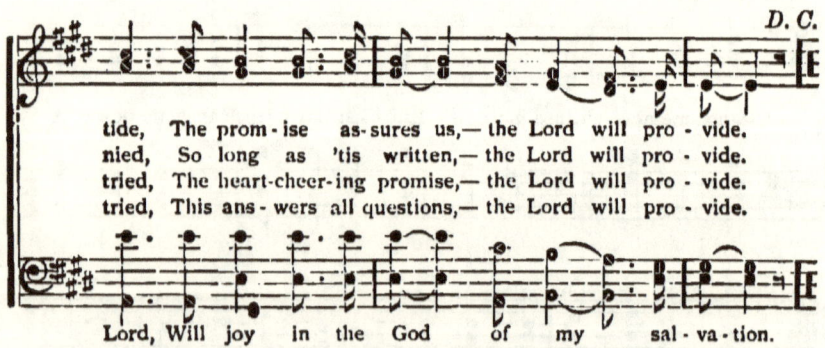

tide, The prom-ise as-sures us,—the Lord will pro-vide.
nied, So long as 'tis written,—the Lord will pro-vide.
tried, The heart-cheer-ing promise,—the Lord will pro-vide.
tried, This ans-wers all questions,—the Lord will pro-vide.

Lord, Will joy in the God of my sal-va-tion.

5 No strength of our own, nor goodness we claim;   [name:
Our trust is all thrown on Jesus' great
In this our strong tower for safety we hide;
The Lord is our power,—the Lord will provide,

6 When life sinks apace, and death is in view,
The word of his grace shall comfort us through:
Not fearing or doubting, with Christ on [our side,
We hope to die shouting,—the Lord will provide,

From "Salvation Echoes," by per.

Is not this the Land of Beulah. 31

ANON.   ARRANGED.

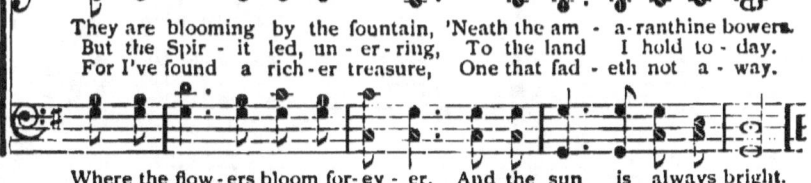

1. I am dwelling on the mountain, Where the golden sunlight gleams
O'er a land whose wondrous beauty Far exceeds my fondest dreams;
Where the air is pure, ethereal, Laden with the breath of flowers,
They are blooming by the fountain, 'Neath the am - aranthine bowers.

2. I can see far down the mountain, Where I wandered weary years,
Often hindered in my journey By the ghosts of doubts and fears,
Broken vows and disappointments Thickly sprinkled all the way,
But the Spirit led, unerring, To the land I hold today.

3. I am drinking at the fountain, Where I ever would abide;
For I've tasted life's pure river, And my soul is satisfied;
There's no thirsting for life's pleasures, Nor adorning, rich and gay,
For I've found a richer treasure, One that fadeth not away.

CHO.—Is not this the land of Beulah, Blessed, blessed land of light,
Where the flowers bloom forever, And the sun is always bright.

4 Tell me not of heavy crosses,
  Nor the burdens hard to bear,
For I've found this great salvation
  Makes each burden light appear;
And I love to follow Jesus,
  Gladly counting all but dross,
Worldly honors all forsaking
  For the glory of the Cross.

5 Oh, the Cross has wondrous glory!
  Oft I've proved this to be true;
When I'm in the way so narrow
  I can see a pathway through;
And how sweetly Jesus whispers:
  Take the Cross, thou need'st not fear
For I've tried this way before thee,
  And the glory lingers near.

The Master's Call.

FANNY J. CROSBY.   WM. F. SHERWIN. By per.

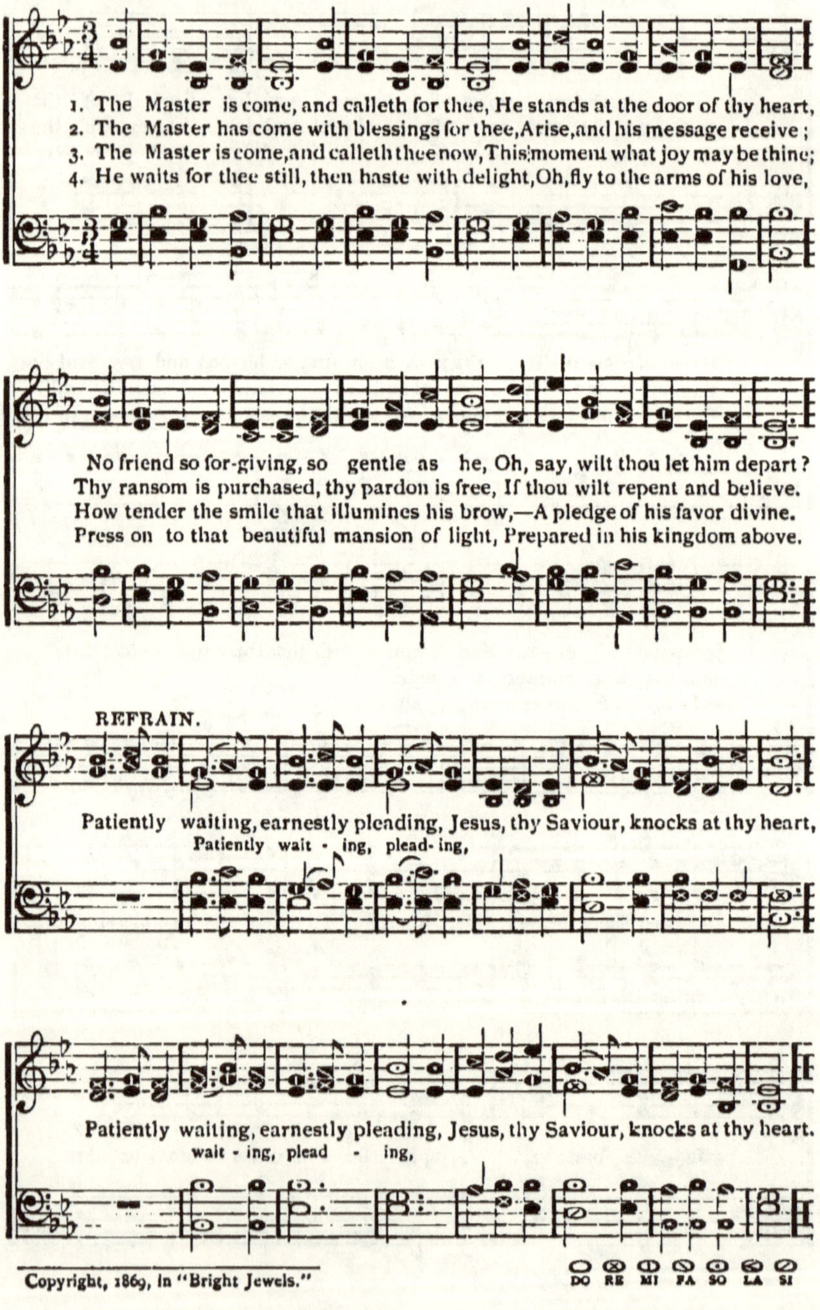

1. The Master is come, and calleth for thee, He stands at the door of thy heart,
2. The Master has come with blessings for thee, Arise, and his message receive;
3. The Master is come, and calleth thee now, This moment what joy may be thine;
4. He waits for thee still, then haste with delight, Oh, fly to the arms of his love,

No friend so for-giving, so gentle as he, Oh, say, wilt thou let him depart?
Thy ransom is purchased, thy pardon is free, If thou wilt repent and believe.
How tender the smile that illumines his brow,—A pledge of his favor divine.
Press on to that beautiful mansion of light, Prepared in his kingdom above.

REFRAIN.

Patiently waiting, earnestly pleading, Jesus, thy Saviour, knocks at thy heart,
Patiently wait - ing, plead- ing,

Patiently waiting, earnestly pleading, Jesus, thy Saviour, knocks at thy heart.
wait - ing, plead - ing,

Copyright, 1869, in "Bright Jewels."

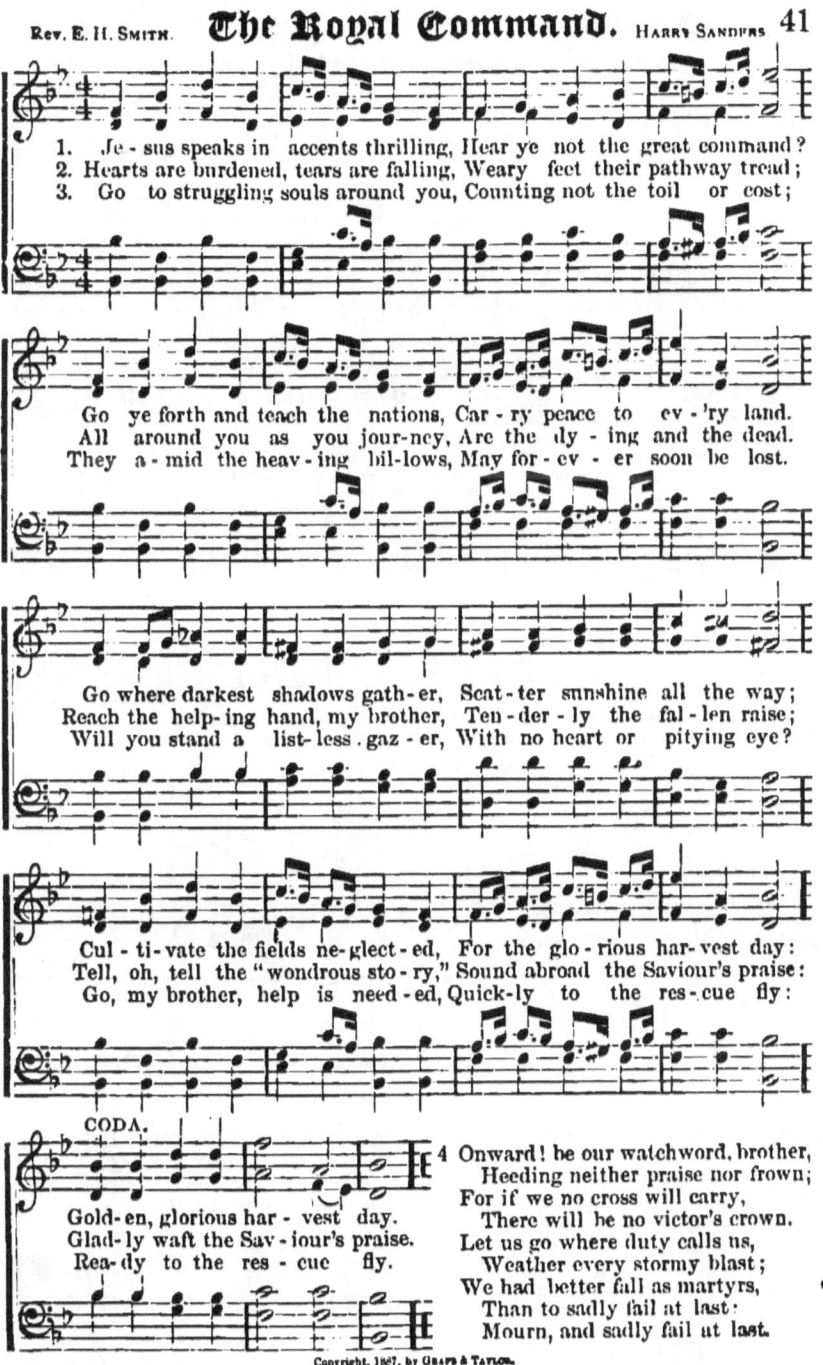

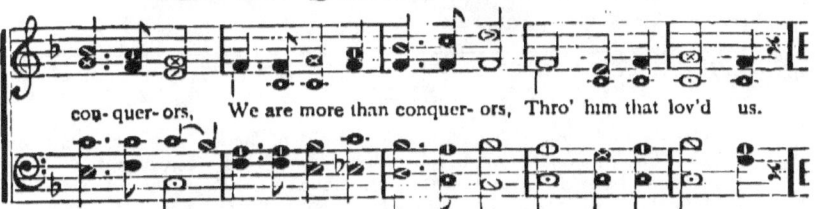

3 Depths that are beneath us,
Heights that are above us,
 Have no power to sunder,
Since he stooped to love us.

Prince of our Redemption,
Sons to glory bringing,
 Thou hast made from sinners
Victors, crowned and singing.—*Cho.*

Light after Darkness.

DUET.   JNO. R. SWENEY.

1. Light af - ter darkness, Gain af - ter loss, Strength af - ter weakness, Crown af - ter cross, Sweet af - ter bit - ter, Song af - ter fears, Home af - ter wander - ing, Praise af - ter tears.
2. Sheaves af - ter sow - ing, Sun af - ter rain, Sight af - ter mys - tery, Peace af - ter pain, Joy af - ter sor - row, Calm af - ter blast, Rest af - ter weari - ness, Sweet rest at last.
3. Near af - ter dis - tant, Gleam af - ter gloom, Love af - ter loneliness, Life af - ter tomb; Af - ter long a - go - ny, Rap - ture of bliss; Right was the path - way Leading to this!

From "Goodly Pearls," by per.

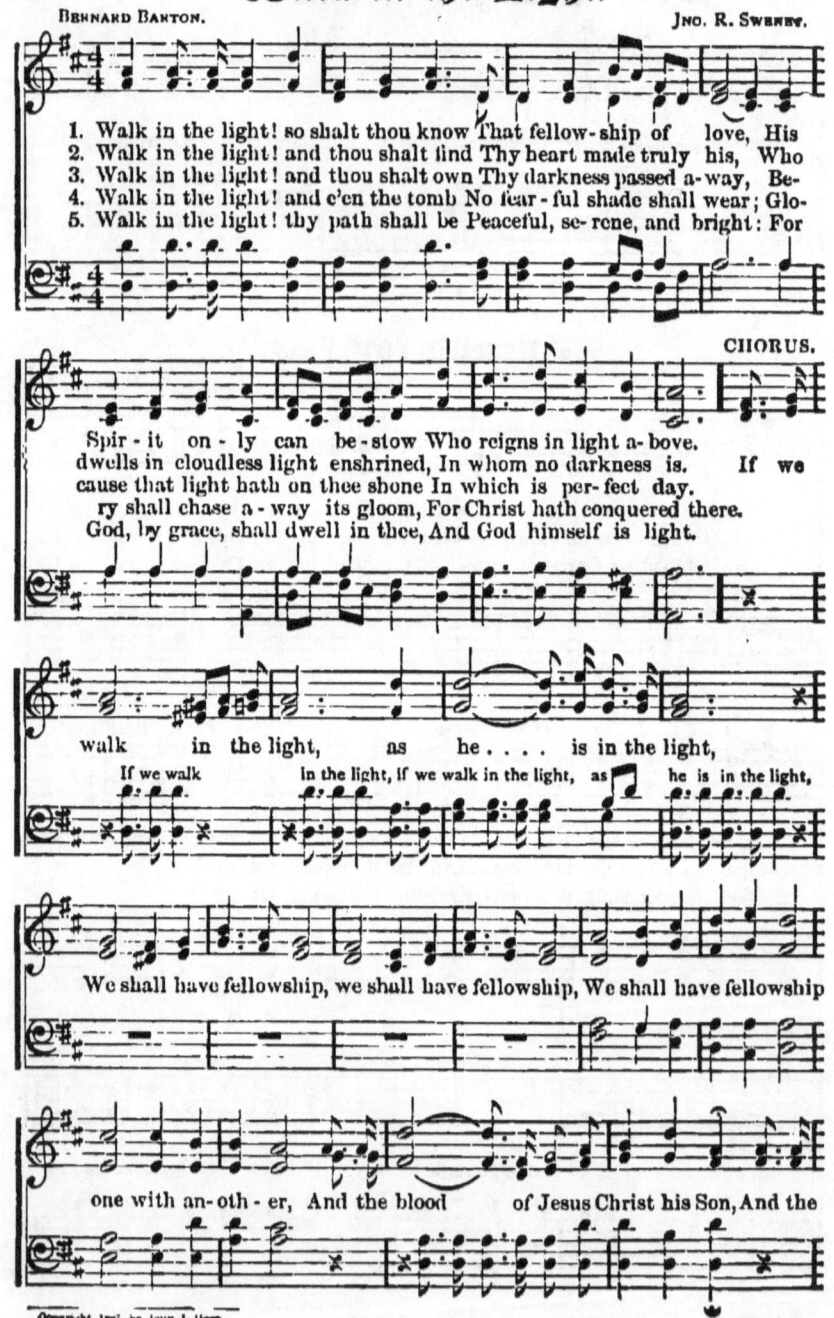

Walk in the Light.—CONCLUDED. 47

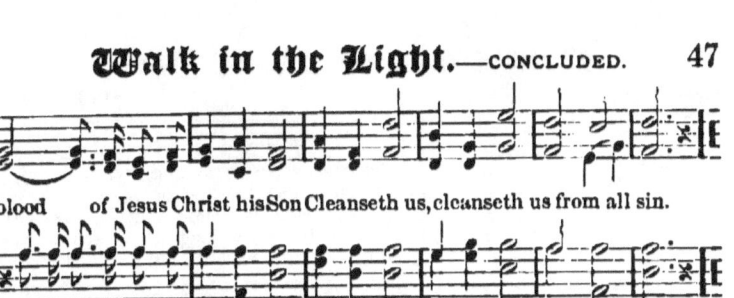

blood of Jesus Christ his Son Cleanseth us, cleanseth us from all sin.

I Bring my Sins to Thee.

F. R. HAVERGAL.   "In returning, . . . ye shall be saved."—Isa. xxx. 15.   JOHN T. GRAPE.

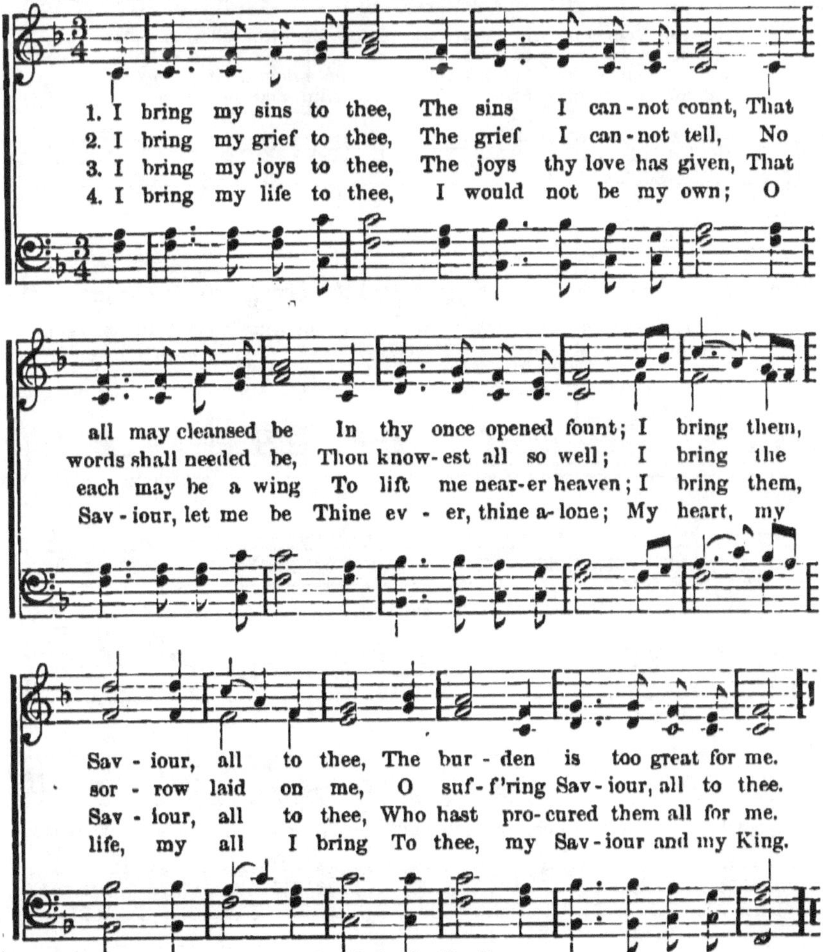

1. I bring my sins to thee, The sins I can-not count, That all may cleansed be In thy once opened fount; I bring them, Sav-iour, all to thee, The bur-den is too great for me.
2. I bring my grief to thee, The grief I can-not tell, No words shall needed be, Thou know-est all so well; I bring the sor-row laid on me, O suf-f'ring Sav-iour, all to thee.
3. I bring my joys to thee, The joys thy love has given, That each may be a wing To lift me near-er heaven; I bring them, Sav-iour, all to thee, Who hast pro-cured them all for me.
4. I bring my life to thee, I would not be my own; O Sav-iour, let me be Thine ev - er, thine a-lone; My heart, my life, my all I bring To thee, my Sav-iour and my King.

From "Pearls of Gospel Song," by per.

54. Lift Up Your Heads.

Mrs. R. N. Turner.
Wm. J. Kirkpatrick.

1. Who is this that cometh strong in might, Strong in glory, great and high?
O ye ev-erlast-ing doors, ye gates, Lift your heads, he draweth nigh!
It is the Lord, the Lord of hosts, He comes with might this way;
With ma-jes-ty, and power, and strength He comes, he comes to-day.

2. Earth with all its fulness is his own, Made by his almight-y hands!
All the seas shall praise his holy name, Floods o-bey his high commands!
They own his power supreme and great, Rejoic-ing to ful-fill,
In raging storm or heavenly calm, His own al-might-y will.

3. Ho-ly are the plac-es where he dwells: Who shall on his work attend?
Who shall dare approach him great in power, And his ho-ly mount as-cend?
Who hath clean hands and undefiled, Who hath pure heart and true,
Let on-ly him draw near the King, And his great glo-ry view.

CHORUS.

Lift up your heads, O ye gates, and be ye lifted up, ye ev-erlasting doors,

Copyright, 1890, by John J. Hood.

Lift Up Your Heads.—CONCLUDED.

And the King of glory shall come in, The King of glory shall come in.

Remember Calvary.

CHAS. WESLEY. WM. J. KIRKPATRICK.

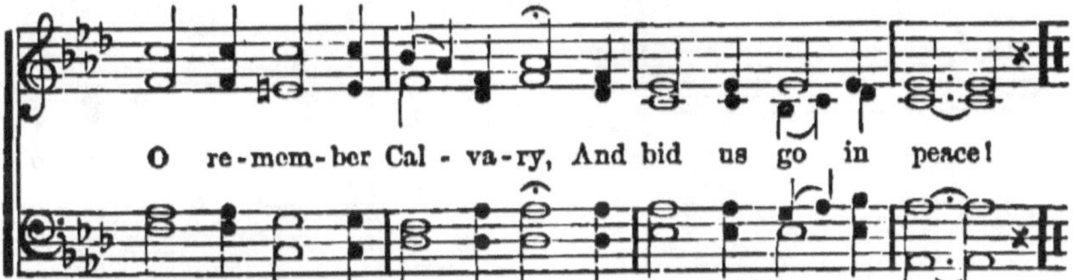

1. Lamb of God, whose dy-ing love We now re-call to mind,
   Send the ans-wer from a-bove, And let us mer-cy find:
   Think on us who think on thee, And ev-'ry struggling soul re-lease;
   O re-mem-ber Cal-va-ry, And bid us go in peace!

2 By thine agonizing pain,
  And bloody sweat, we pray,
  By thy dying love to man,
  Take all our sins away.
  Burst our bonds, and set us free;
  From all iniquity release;
  O remember Calvary,
  And bid us go in peace!

3 Let thy blood, by faith applied,
  The sinner's pardon seal;
  Speak us freely justified,
  And all our sickness heal:
  By thy passion on the tree,
  Let all our griefs and troubles [cease:
  O remember Calvary,
  And bid us go in peace!

Copyright, 1895, by JOHN J. HOOD.

DO RE MI FA SO LA SI

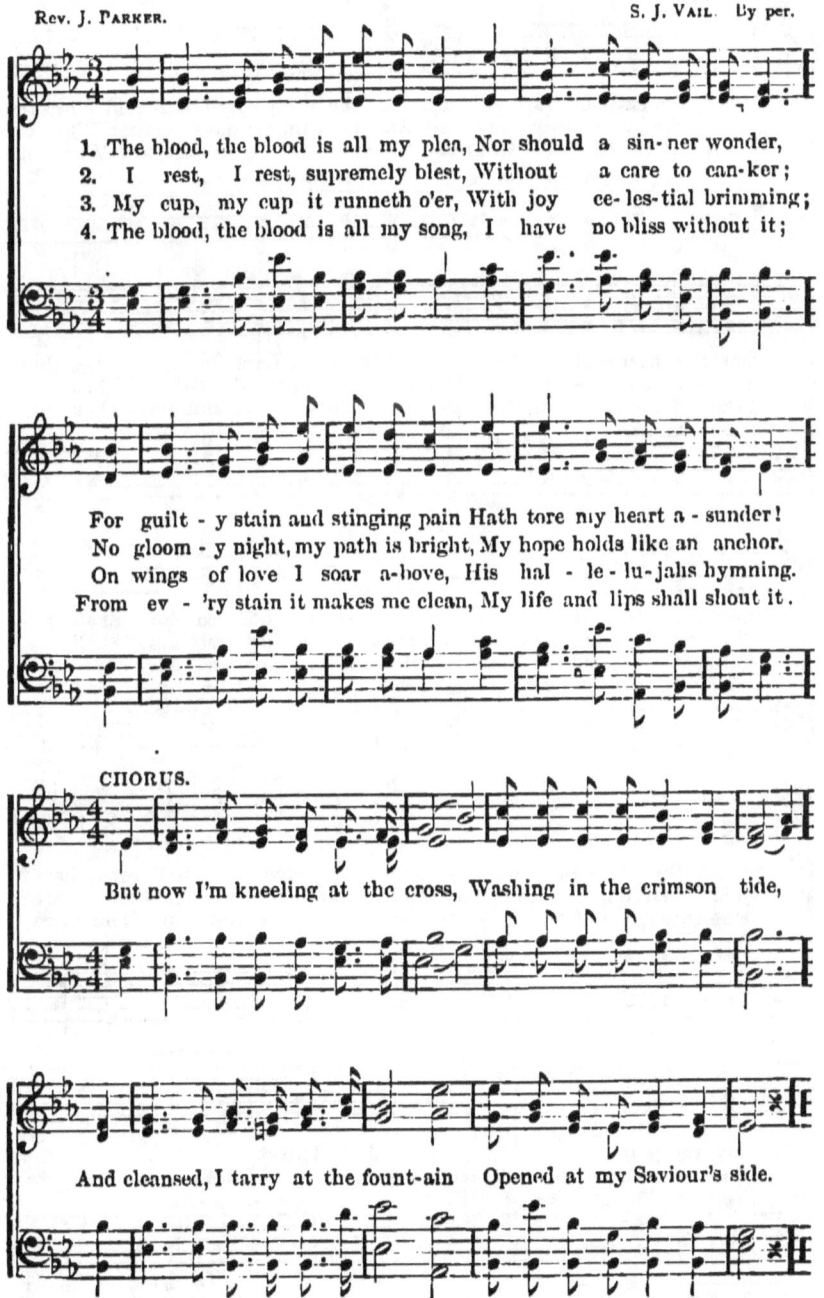

By the Grace of God, etc.—CONCLUDED. 59

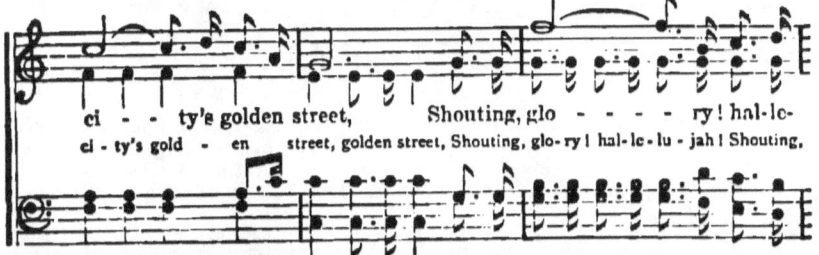

C. J. B.   **A Sinner like Me.**   CHAS. J. BUTLER.

2 I wandered on in the darkness,
   Not a ray of light could I see, [ness,
   And the thought filled my heart with sad-
   There's no hope for a sinner like me.

3 I then fully trusted in Jesus,
   And oh, what a joy came to me;
   My heart was filled with his praises,
   For saving a sinner like me.

4 No longer in darkness I'm walking,
   For the light is now shining on me,
   And now unto others I'm telling,
   How he saved a poor sinner like me.

5 And when life's journey is over,
   And I the dear Saviour shall see,
   I'll praise him forever and ever,
   For saving a sinner like me.

Copyright, 1881, by JOHN J. HOOD.

1 The God of Abrah'm praise,
  Who reigns enthroned above,
Ancient of everlasting days,
  And God of love:
Jehovah, great I Am,
  By earth and heav'n confessed;
I bow and bless the sacred name,
  Forever blest.

2 The God of Abrah'm praise,
  At whose supreme command
From earth I rise, and seek the joys
  At his right hand:
I all on earth forsake,
  Its wisdom, fame, and power;
And him my only portion make,
  My shield and tower.

3 The God of Abrah'm praise,
  Whose all-sufficient grace
Shall guide me, all my happy days,
  In all his ways;
He calls a worm his friend,
  He calls himself my God!
And he shall save me to the end,
  Through Jesus' blood.

4 He by Himself hath sworn,
  I on his oath depend;
I shall, on eagle wings upborne,
  To heaven ascend;
I shall behold his face,
  I shall his power adore,
And sing the wonders of his grace
  For evermore.

66. The Lily of the Valley.

English Melody, arranged

1. I have found a friend in Jesus, he's ev'rything to me, He's the fairest of ten thousand to my soul; The Lily of the Valley, in him alone I see All I need to cleanse and make me fully whole; In sorrow he's my comfort, in trouble he's my stay, He tells me ev'ry care on him to roll.

2. He all my griefs has taken, and all my sorrows borne; In temptation he's my strong and mighty tower; I have all for him forsaken, and all my idols torn From my heart, and now he keeps me by his power; Tho' all the world forsake me, and Satan tempts me sore, Thro' Jesus I shall safely reach the goal.

3. He will never, never leave me, nor yet forsake me here, While I live by faith and do his blessed will; A wall of fire about me, I've nothing now to fear; With his manna he my hungry soul shall fill; Then sweeping up to glory to see his blessed face, Where rivers of delight shall ever roll.

CHO.—In sorrow, etc. *(after each verse.)*

D. S.—Lily of the Valley, the bright and Morning Star, He's the fairest of ten thousand to my soul.

Copyright, 1885, by JOHN J. HOOD.

One by One.

Rev. E. H. Stokes, D. D. Jno. R. Sweney.

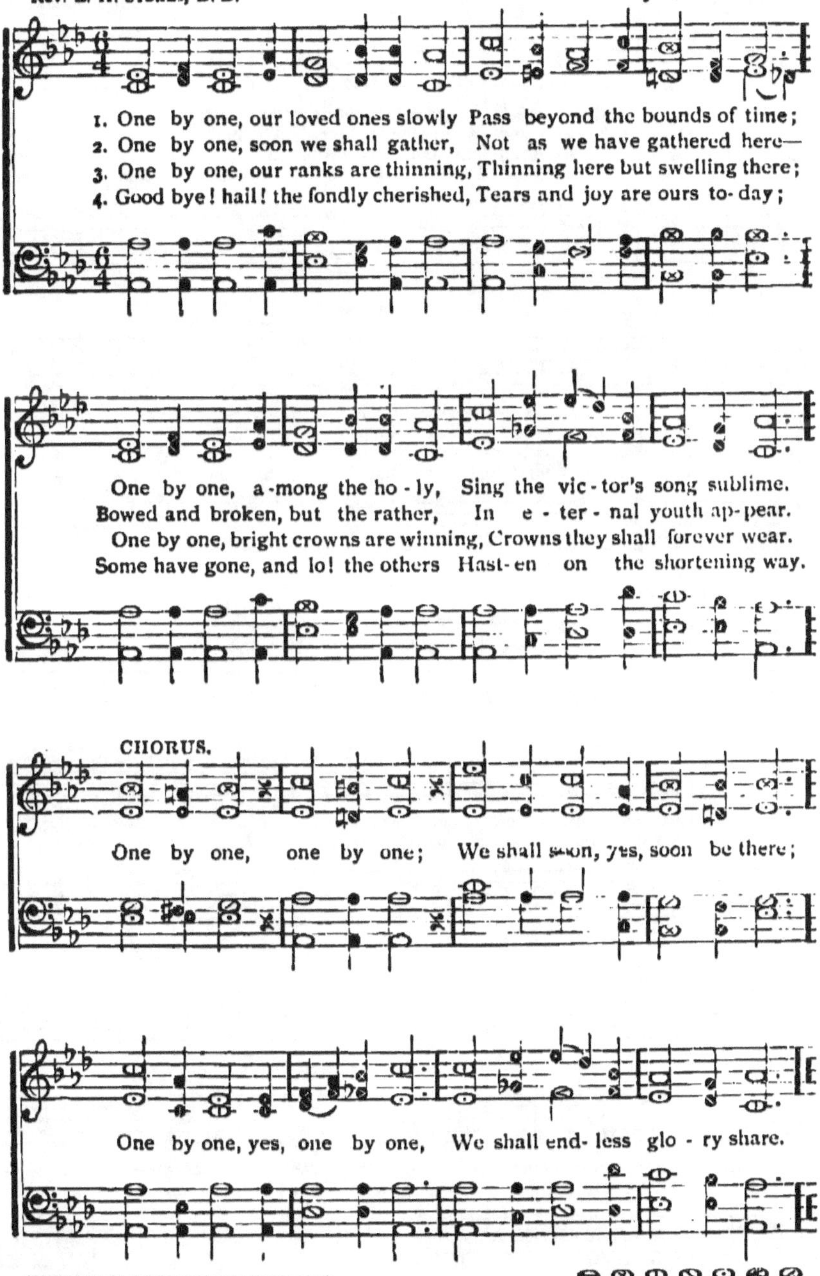

1. One by one, our loved ones slowly Pass beyond the bounds of time;
2. One by one, soon we shall gather, Not as we have gathered here—
3. One by one, our ranks are thinning, Thinning here but swelling there;
4. Good bye! hail! the fondly cherished, Tears and joy are ours to-day;

One by one, a-mong the ho-ly, Sing the vic-tor's song sublime.
Bowed and broken, but the rather, In e-ter-nal youth ap-pear.
One by one, bright crowns are winning, Crowns they shall forever wear.
Some have gone, and lo! the others Hast-en on the shortening way.

CHORUS.

One by one, one by one; We shall soon, yes, soon be there;

One by one, yes, one by one, We shall end-less glo-ry share.

Copyright, 1862, by John J. Hood.

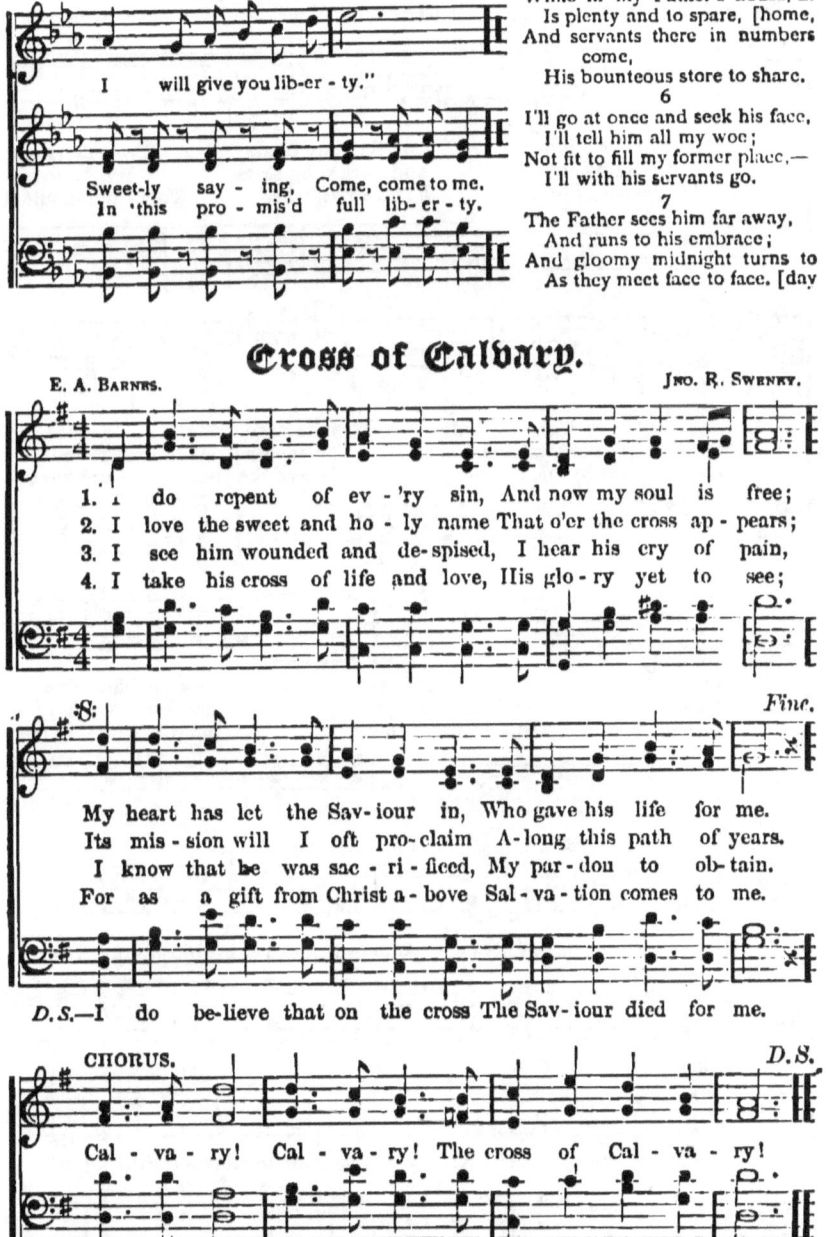

I'm Holding On.

James Nicholson.   Jno. R. Sweney.

1. Tho' weak my faith, I'm holding on; To Jesus I am clinging;
2. I'm holding on, tho' Satan tries To keep me from believing;
3. While holding on by faith I see The blood of Jesus flowing;
4. I'm clinging, clinging, holding on, My faith is rising higher,
5. I'm holding on, and while I make A perfect consecration,

I feel that now the "Mighty One" Help to my soul is bringing.
But, while my soul on God relies, The blessing I'm receiving.
The healing stream is touching me, New life and peace bestowing.
The last remains of sin are gone; I have my heart's desire.
The Holy Ghost, for Jesus' sake, Brings in complete salvation.

CHORUS.

I'm holding on, I'm holding on, Fresh strength each moment gaining,
My ling'ring doubts at last are gone, And Christ within is reigning.

DO RE MI FA SO LA MI

Copyright, 1882, by John J. Hood.

We Shall Know.

Annie Herbert. — J. H. Anderson.

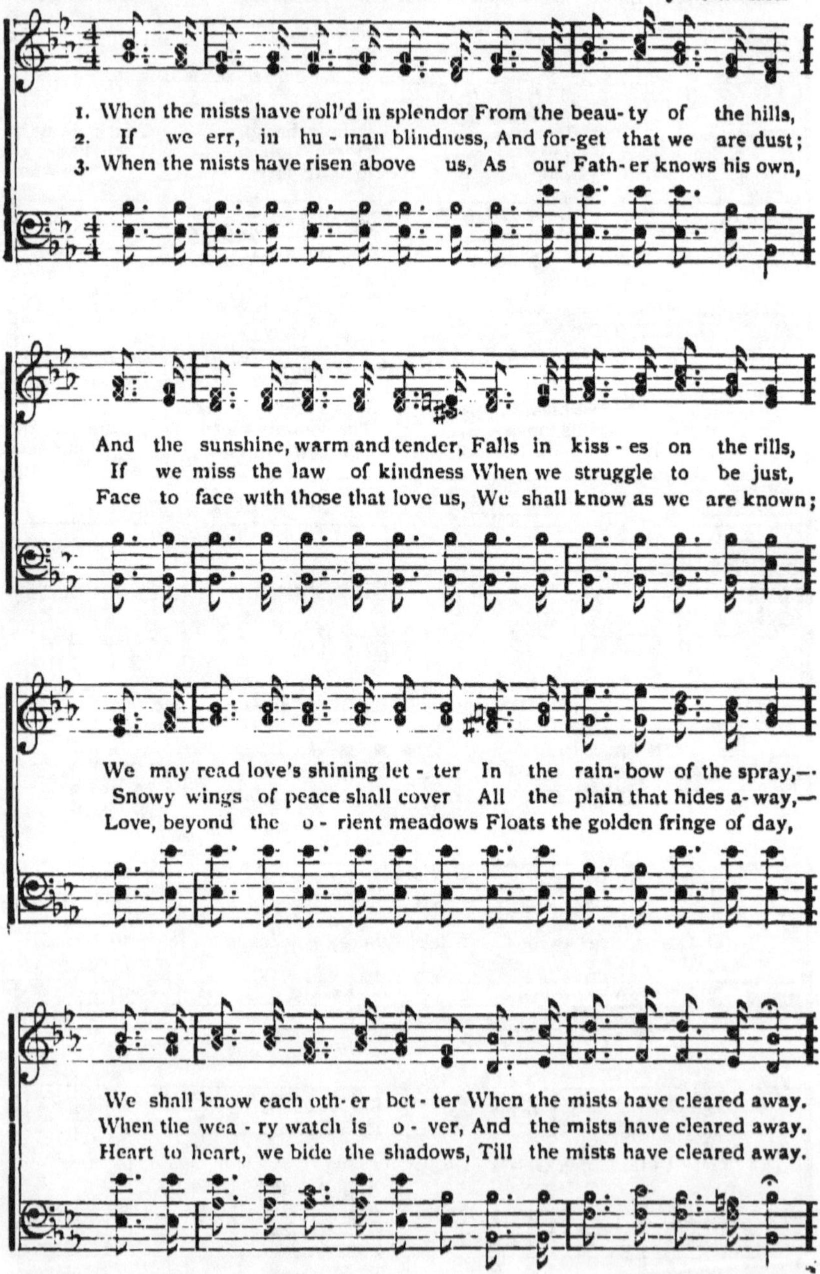

1. When the mists have roll'd in splendor From the beauty of the hills,
And the sunshine, warm and tender, Falls in kisses on the rills,
We may read love's shining letter In the rainbow of the spray,—
We shall know each other better When the mists have cleared away.

2. If we err, in human blindness, And forget that we are dust;
If we miss the law of kindness When we struggle to be just,
Snowy wings of peace shall cover All the plain that hides away,—
When the weary watch is over, And the mists have cleared away.

3. When the mists have risen above us, As our Father knows his own,
Face to face with those that love us, We shall know as we are known;
Love, beyond the orient meadows Floats the golden fringe of day,
Heart to heart, we bide the shadows, Till the mists have cleared away.

From "The Welcome," by per.

We Shall Know.—CONCLUDED.

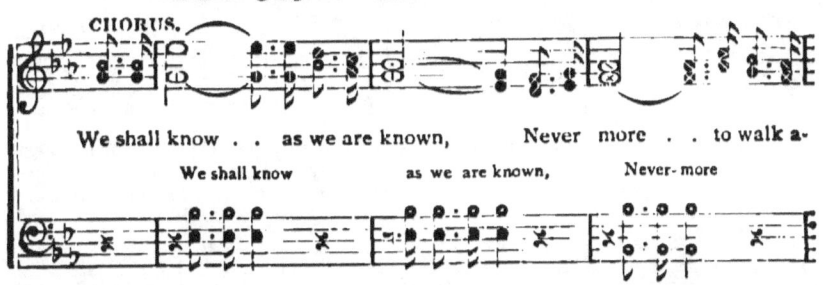

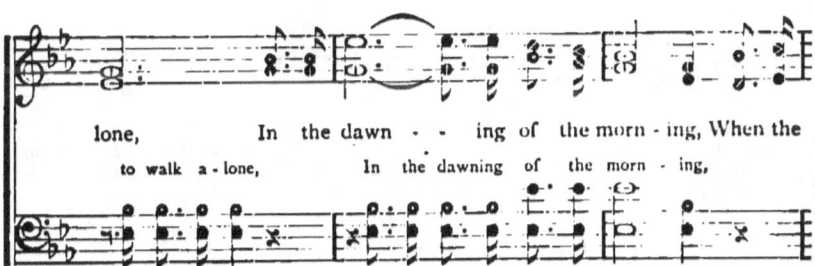

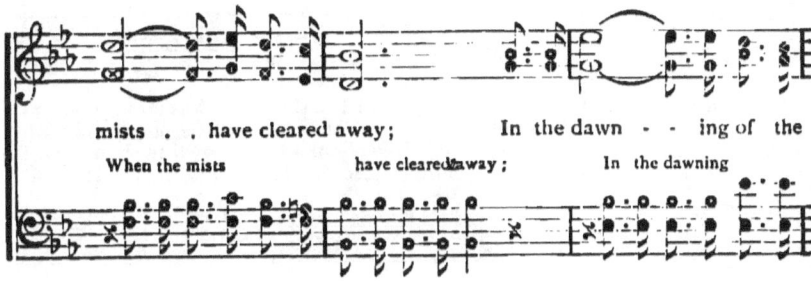

That Old, Old Story is True.—CONCLUDED. 79

found out the reason they love it so well, That old, old sto-ry is true.
oh, what sweet peace in my heart since I found That old, old sto-ry is true.
peace to my soul, it is joy to my heart That old, old sto-ry is true.
mansion in glo-ry for all who beleive" That old, old sto-ry is true.

REFRAIN.

That old, old sto-ry is true, That old, old sto-ry is true; But I've
That old, old sto-ry is true, That old, old sto-ry is true; But
That old, old sto-ry is true, That old, old sto-ry is true; It is
That old, old sto-ry is true, That old, old sto-ry is true; "There's a
          it is true,   it is true,

found out the reason they love it so well, That old, old sto-ry is true.
oh, what sweet peace in my heart since I've found That old, old story is true.
peace to my soul, it is joy to my heart, That old, old sto-ry is true.
mansion in glo-ry for all who believe" That old, old sto-ry is true.

Home of the Soul.   Key Eb.

1 I will sing you a song of a beautiful land,
    The far-away home of the soul,
  Where no storms ever beat on the glittering strand,
    While the years of eternity roll. etc.

2 Oh, that home of the soul in my visions and dreams,
    Its bright, jasper walls I can see;
  Till I fancy but thinly the veil intervenes
    Between the fair city and me. etc.

3 That unchangeable home is for you and for me,
    Where Jesus of Nazareth stands;
  The King of all kingdoms forever is he,
    And he holdeth our crowns in his hands. etc.

4 Oh, how sweet it will be in that beautiful land,
    So free from all sorrow and pain,
  With songs on our lips, and with harps in our hands,
    To meet one another again. etc.

80. I Hope to Meet You All in Glory.

EMMA PITT. [From "Our Sabbath Home," by per.] WM. J. KIRKPATRICK.

1. I hope to meet you all in glo-ry, When the storms of life are o'er;
2. I hope to meet you all in glo-ry, By the tree of life so fair;
3. I hope to meet you all in glo-ry, Round the Saviour's throne above;
4. I hope to meet you all in glo-ry, When my work on earth is o'er;

I hope to tell the dear old sto-ry, On the bles-sed shin-ing shore.
I hope to praise our dear Redeem-er For the grace that brought me there.
I hope to join the ransomed arm-y Singing now redeem-ing love.
I hope to clasp your hands rejoic-ing On the bright e-ter-nal shore.

CHORUS.

On the shin-ing shore, On the gold-en strand, In our Father's home, In the hap-py land: I hope to meet you there, I hope to meet you there,—A crown of vict-'ry wear,—In glo-ry.

Copyright, 1884, by JOHN J. HOOD.

Ecce Homo. 81

Prof. T. D. Baird, Ph. D.

1. All ye who pass by, To Jesus draw nigh; To you is it nothing that Jesus should die? Our Ransom and Peace, Our Surety he is, Come, see if there ever was sorrow like his, Come, see if there ever was sorrow like his.
2. The Lord in the day Of his anger did lay Our sins on the Lamb, and he bore them away; He died to atone For guilt not his own! The Father afflicted for us his dear Son, The Father afflicted for us his dear Son.
3. For sinners like me He died on the tree; His death is accepted, the sinner goes free! My pardon I claim; A sinner I am, A sinner believing in Jesus' dear name, A sinner believing in Jesus' dear name.
4. With joy we approve The plan of his love, A wonder to all, both below and above, When time is no more, We still shall adore The ocean of love without bottom or shore, The ocean of love without bottom or shore.

Emory Hymnal—F Copyright, 1887, by Grape & Taylor.

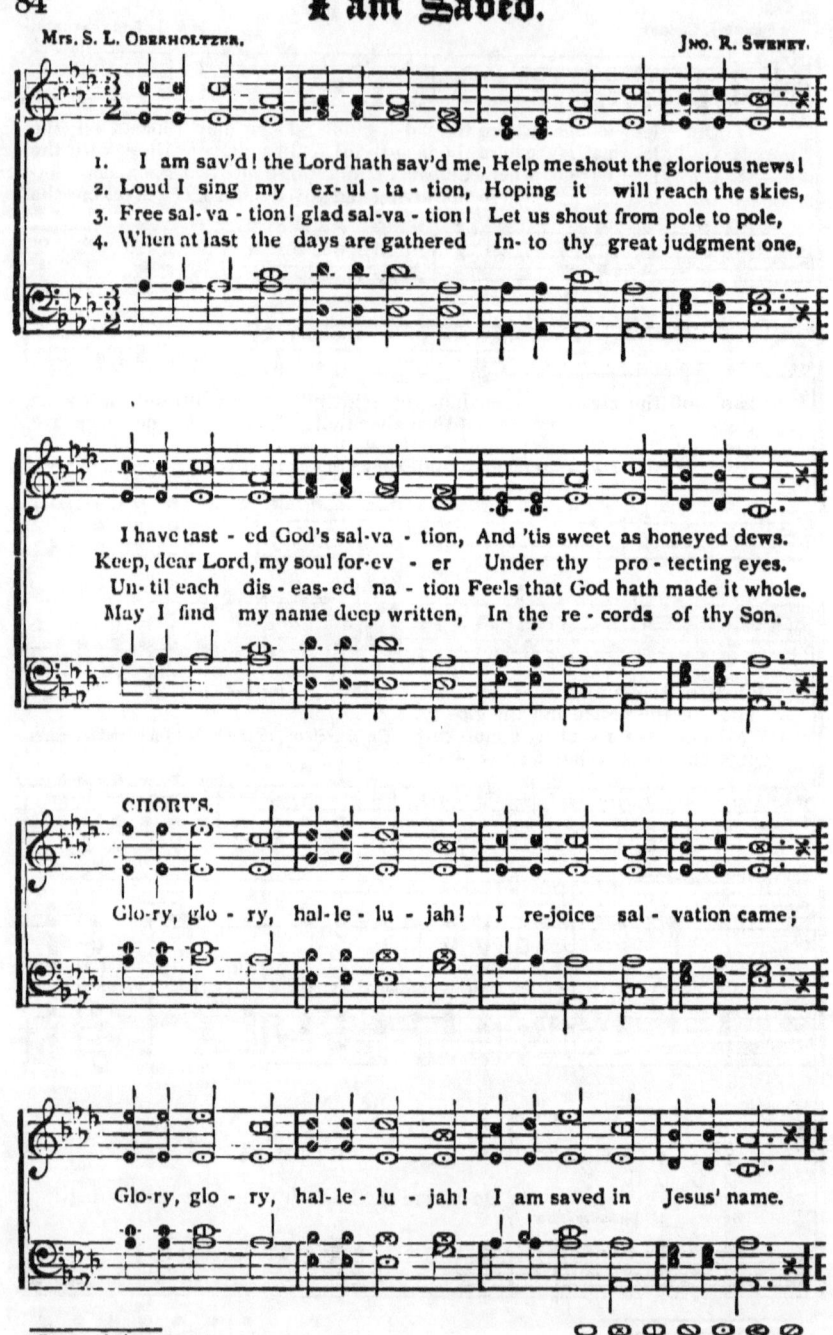

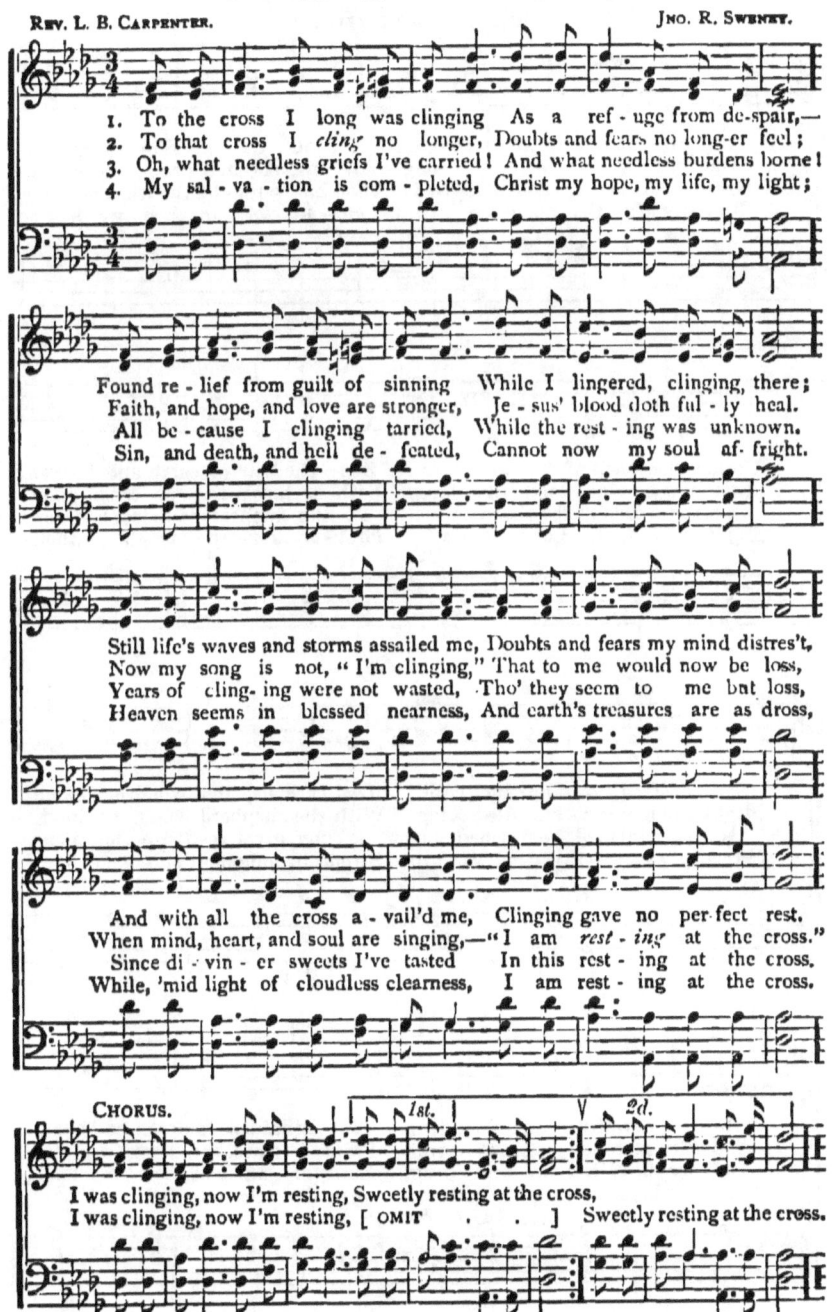

Mighty to Save.

2 O why is thine apparel
  With reeking gore all dyed,
Like them that tread the winepress red?
  O why this bloody tide?
" I the winepress trod alone,
  'Neath darkening skies;
Of the people there was none
  Mighty to save."

3 O bleeding Lamb, my Saviour,
  How couldst thou bear this shame?
" With mercy fraught, mine own arm
  Salvation in my name;   [brought
I the bloody fight have won,
  Conquered the grave,
Now the year of joy has come,—
  Mighty to save."

Christ Shall Reign.—CONCLUDED. 93

Le. Edwards. Christmas Carol.—Hope's Bright Star.   Tune above.

1 Hail, hail, hail, beautiful sky, beautiful sky,
Yonder comes the queen of morning,
  Night is gliding by;
Over the world once more, folding her wings, folding her wings,
Peace, her gentle harp awaking,
  Smiles and sings.
Sweet as when the joyful tidings
‖: Sounded long ago, :‖   [them
Sweet as when the shepherds heard
‖: Still their numbers flow, :‖
Unto us is born a Saviour,
  He is born to-day;
Come, behold the meek and lowly,
  Come quickly away.

Chorus.—
Hail, hail, hail, beautiful light, beautiful
  Thro' the birth of our Redeemer [light,

Making all so bright;   [ing afar,
Beautiful light of God, shining afar, shin-
Every eye may see its glory,
  Hope's bright star.
2 Come, come, come, tripping along trip-
Carol o'er the sacred story [ping along,
  All have loved so long;
List to the chiming bells, merry and clear,
  merry and clear,
Happy Christmas, happy Christmas,
  Welcome, welcome here.
Graceful boughs of green are waving,
‖: Hearts with rapture beat, :‖
Love and mercy bending o'er us
‖: Precious words repeat, :‖
Where the royal Prince of glory
  In a manger lay,
Faith will lead and gently guide us,
  Come quickly away.

From "Hood's Carols for— —Christmas, No. 6," by per.

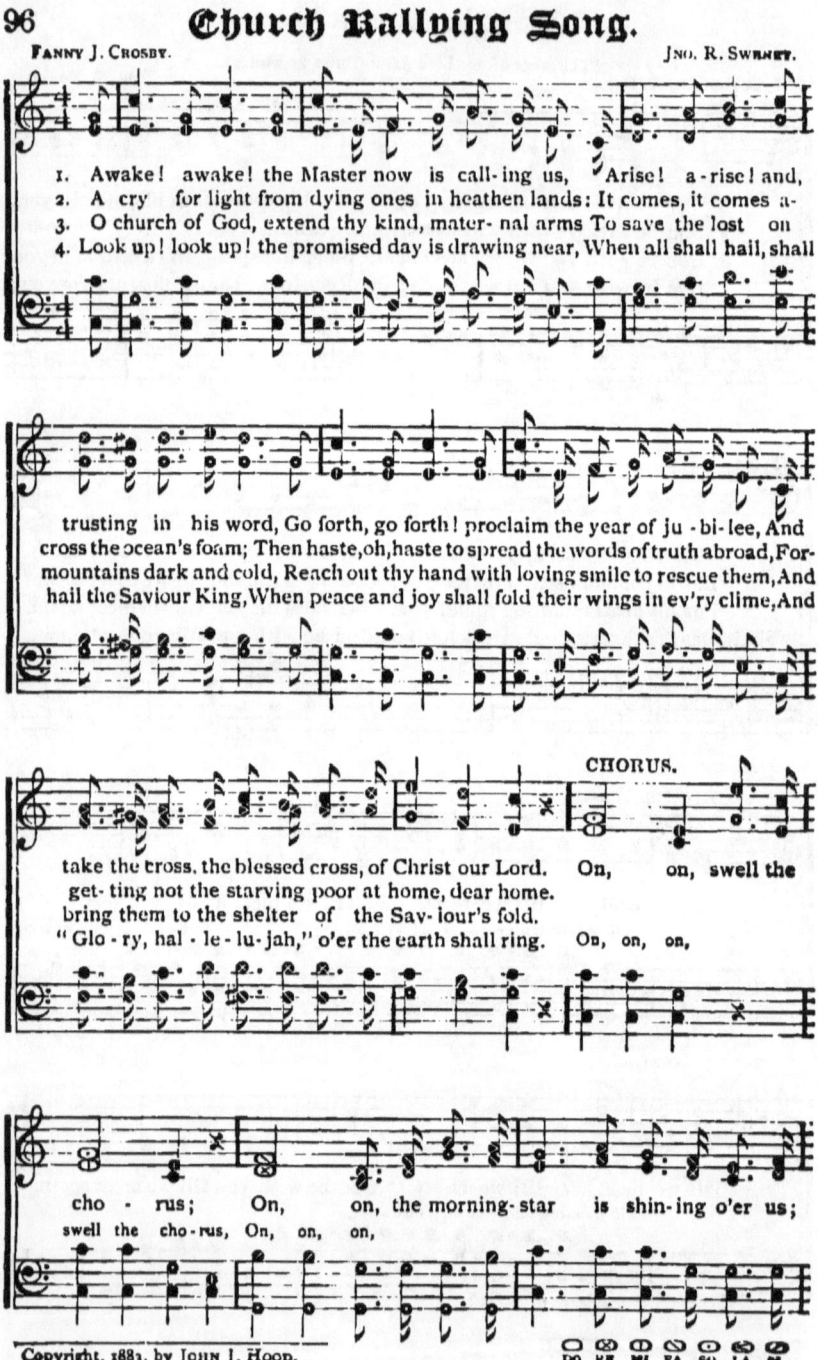

Church Rallying Song.—CONCLUDED.

On, on, while before us Our mighty, mighty Saviour leads the way:
On, on, on, while be-fore leads the way:

Glo - ry, glo - ry, hear the ev - erlasting throng } Faithful soldiers here below,
Shout ho- sanna, while we boldly march along;

On - ly Jesus will we know, Shouting "free salvation" o'er the world we go.

F J. C.   **Christmas Carol.—Awake! awake!**   Tune above.

1 Awake! awake! our festive day is dawning now,
Awake! awake! and hail its golden light;
Rejoice! rejoice! behold the Sun of Righteousness
Arising in its beauty o'er a long, long night.

Cho.—Come, come, join the chorus,
Come, come, the angel hosts are bending o'er us;
Come, come, join the chorus,—
All glory be to God, to God above.
Oh, the rapture of the bright angelic form,
Oh, the rapture while the anthem rolls along.
Hark! the merry, merry bells,
Everywhere their music swells;
Hark! the merry chiming of the grand old bells.

3 Good news, good news resounding o'er the earth again,
Good news, good news: behold a Saviour born;
Make room, make room in every heart to welcome him,
And shout aloud, hosanna! on his birthday morn.

4 He comes, he comes, the captive's cruel chain to break,
He comes, he comes to give his people rest;
Break forth, break forth, his mighty, mighty love proclaim;
In him shall every nation, every clime, be blessed.

From "Hood's Carols," by per.] G

DO RE MI FA SO LA SI

4 Let us live for one another,
　　Help a little, help a little;
　Help to lift each fallen brother,
　　Help just a little.

5 Tho' thy life is pressed with sorrow,
　　Help a little, help a little;
　Bravely look t'ward God's to-morrow,
　　Help just a little.

Copyright, 1885, by John J. Hood.

Looking unto Jesus.—CONCLUDED. 105

Looking un-to Je-sus, O-ver all the armor Faith the battle shield.

I will Trust in Thee.

In answer to question of leader at Ocean Grove "Who will trust?" many rose, saying, "I will."

W. H. G. W. H. GRISTWRIT.

1. Blessed Saviour, my sal-vation, I will trust in thee; I am saved from
2. Sanctify and cleanse me, Saviour, I will trust in thee; Let me know thy
3. Here I stand and thee confessing, I will trust in thee; Pour up-on my

CHORUS.

condemn-a-tion, I will trust in thee. Yes, I will, yes, I will,
lov-ing fa-vor, I will trust in thee.
heart thy blessing, I will trust in thee.

I will trust in thee; Thou, my Strength and Song forever, I will trust in thee.

Copyright, 1896, by JOHN J. HOOD.

Rest.

Rev. E. H. Stokes, D. D.
With feeling.
Jno. R. Sweney.

1. Touch my spir-it with thy Spir-it, Lord of All, my Sav-iour;
2. I have found him, what a treasure!—Found my blessed Sav-iour;
3. I have found him: past my weeping, Blessed, bles-sed Sav-iour;

Let me thy sweet rest in-her-it, This my high-est fa-vor.
This the pleasure of all pleasures, Rest in my dear Sav-iour.
And my soul to thy kind keep-ing I com-mit, dear Sav-iour.

CHORUS.

Rest, sweet rest, rest, sweet rest In my bles-sed Sav-iour;

Rest, sweet rest, rest, sweet rest In my bles-sed Sav-iour.

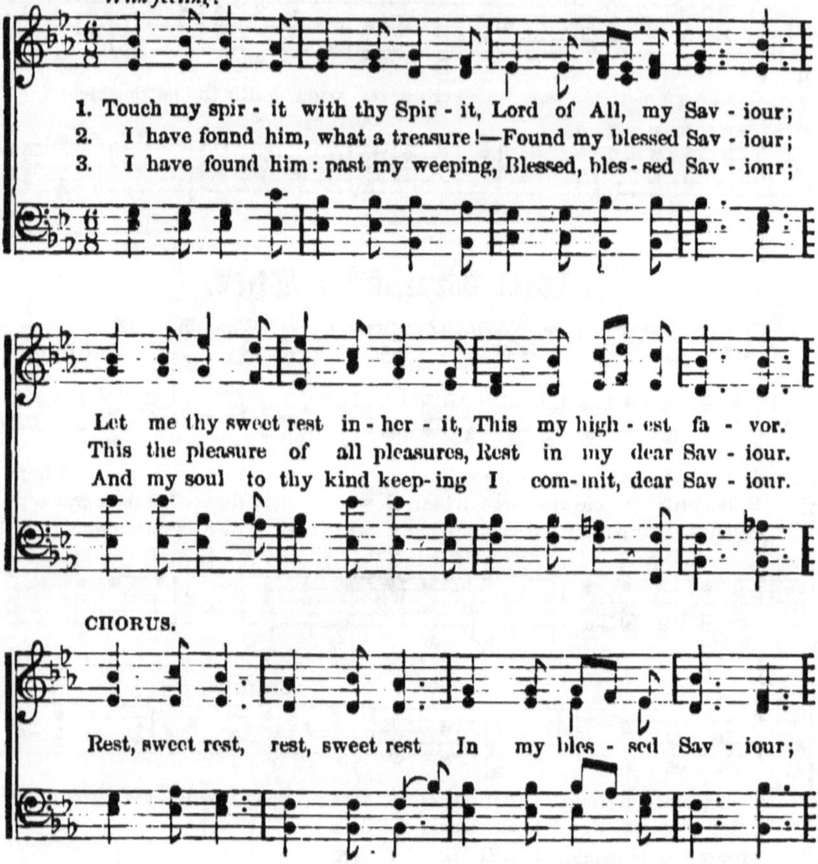

4 On the earth this heavenly resting
   Comes to me, dear Saviour;
  This is love's own manifesting,
   Through my blessed Saviour.

5 In this rest toil does not weary,—
   Toil for thee, my Saviour;
  In the gloom there's nothing dreary,
   With thee, O my Saviour.

Copyright, 1885, by John J. Hood.

4 Temptations hard upon me press:
  No strength is mine, I know:
Yet more than conqueror am I—
  Jesus saves me now!

5 Whate'er my future may require,
  His grace will sure allow;
I live one moment at a time,
  Jesus saves me now!

6 Why doubt him? He who died now lives;
  The crown is on his brow;
The Son of Man hath power on earth:
  Jesus saves me now.

7 And when within the pearly gates
  I at his feet shall bow,
The heaven of heavens itself will be:
  Jesus saves me now.

108. Unto him that hath loved us.

Rev. E. H. Smith.   H. Sanders. By per.

1. I have giv'n my all to Je-sus, And I live where the light doth shine; In the
2. I was once in darkness groping, I once roamed in the desert wild; But the
3. To the cooling fount he led me, To the pastures ev-er green; And my

world's deep gloom my hopes ever bloom, There is peace in this heart of mine.
Lord passed by, pouring light on my eye, And reclaimed me, his wand'ring child.
soul is restored, and shall boast in her Lord, For his blood hath washed me clean.

ff Chorus.

Un-to him that hath loved us, and washed ev'-ry stain, Un-to him the do-
minion and glo-ry be giv'n; O'er the world he shall come in his beauty to reign,
As he reigns in the brightness of heav'n.

4.
My faith, as the eagle, mounteth
On her pinion bold and strong;
And the world beneath is the sadness of
But above is immortal song. [death,

5.
O swift are the moments speeding,
And the land that is far away
Soon, soon shall be mine! and its morn-
Will dawn an eternal day, [ing divine

4 Let me no wrong or idle word
　　Unthinking say;
　Set thou a seal upon my lips
　　Just for to-day.

5 So for to-morrow and its needs
　　I do not pray;
　Keep me and guide me, hold me, Lord,
　　Just for to-day.

Look and Live. 113

"And the Lord said unto Moses, Make thee a fiery serpent, and set it upon a pole; and it shall come to pass that every one that is bitten, when he looketh upon it, shall live."

F. E. B.   Num. xxi. 8.   F. E. Belden.

Tenderly.

1. Look to the cross, sin-ner, believe it; Look to the cross, healing is there;
2. Leave all thy sin, humbly confess - ing, Truly forsake, turn and o - bey;
3. Ask of the Lord, now he is willing Strength to impart, grace to bestow;
4. Look to the cross, trusting in Je - sus, Mighty to help, mighty to save;

Pardon is thine, on - ly receive it; Look to the cross in prayer.
Je - sus will give free - ly his blessing,—Ask and receive to - day.
Prom-is - es sweet, ev - er ful - fill - ing, Prove the great debt we owe.
From all our guilt glad - ly he frees us, For us his life he gave.

CHORUS.

Look to the cross, look to the cross, Jesus believ - ing, pardon receiv - ing;

Look to the cross, look to the cross, Look, and thy soul shall live.

Emory Hymnal—H   Copyright, 1800, by F. E. Belden.

I shall be Satisfied.

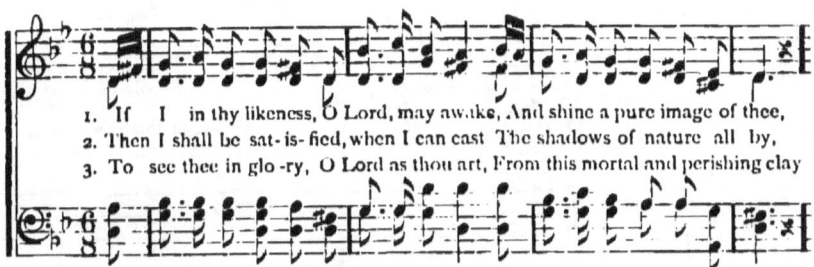

1. If I in thy likeness, O Lord, may awake, And shine a pure image of thee,
2. Then I shall be sat-is-fied, when I can cast The shadows of nature all by,
3. To see thee in glo-ry, O Lord as thou art, From this mortal and perishing clay

Then I shall be sat-is-fied when I can break These fetters of flesh and be free;
When this cold, dreary world from my vision is past, To let this soul o-pen her eye;
The spir-it immortal in peace would depart, And joyous mount up her bright way

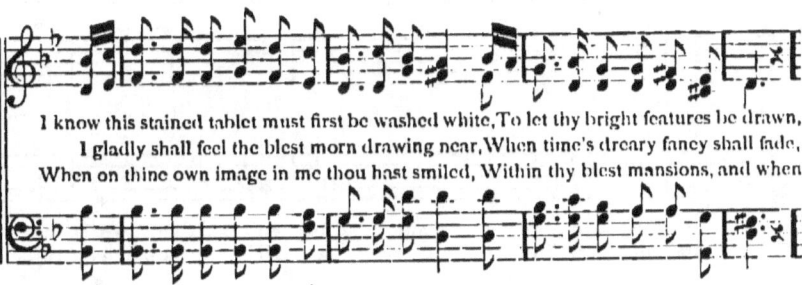

I know this stained tablet must first be washed white, To let thy bright features be drawn,
I gladly shall feel the blest morn drawing near, When time's dreary fancy shall fade,
When on thine own image in me thou hast smiled, Within thy blest mansions, and when

I know I must suffer the darkness of night To welcome the coming of dawn.
If then in thy likeness I may but appear, And rise with thy beauty arrayed.
The arms of my Father en-cir-cle his child, Oh, I shall be sat-is-fied then.

— CONCLUDED.

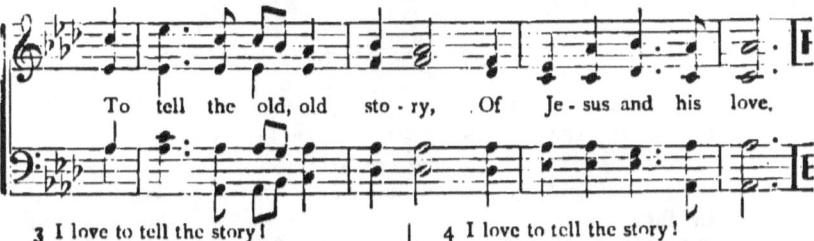

3 I love to tell the story!
    'Tis pleasant to repeat
  What seems, each time I tell it,
    More wonderfully sweet.
  I love to tell the story;
    For some have never heard
  The message of salvation
    From God's own Holy Word.

4 I love to tell the story!
    For those who know it best
  Seem hungering and thirsting
    To hear it like the rest.
  And when, in scenes of glory,
    I sing the *New, New Song*,
  'Twill be the *Old, Old Story*,
    That I have loved so long.

MRS. E. CODNER.   **Even Me.**   JNO. R. SWENEY.

1. Lord, I hear of showers of blessing, Thou art scatt'ring full and free—
2. Pass me not, O gracious Father! Sin-ful tho' my heart may be;
3. Pass me not, O tender Saviour! Let me live and cling to thee;

Showers, the thirst-y land re-freshing; Let some droppings fall on me.—
Thou might'st leave me, but the rath-er Let thy mer-cy fall on me.—
I am long-ing for thy fa-vor; Whilst thou'rt calling, oh, call me.—

E-ven me, Yes, e-ven me, E-ven me, yes, e-ven me.—

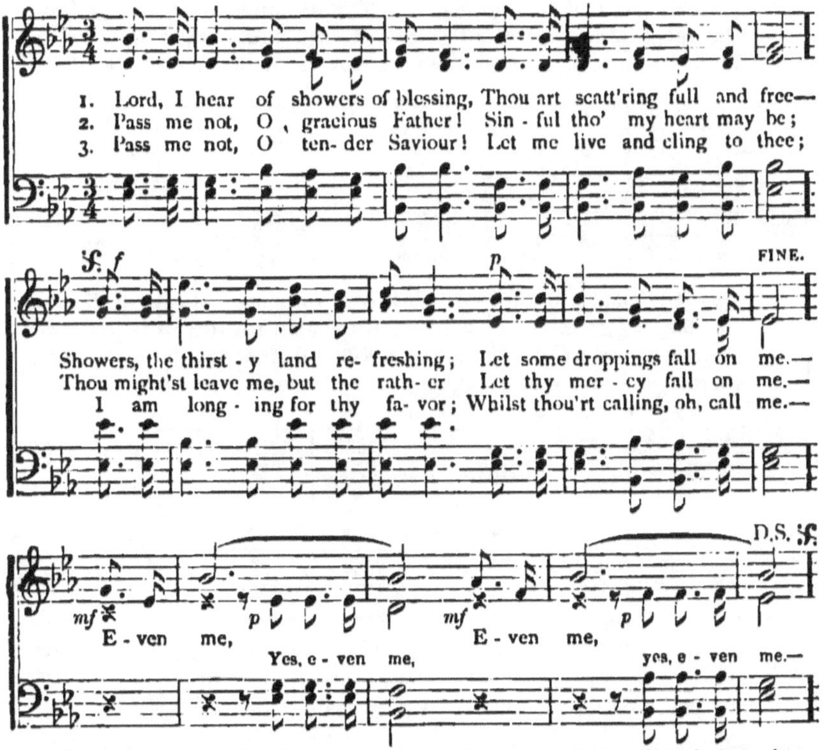

4 Pass me not, O mighty Spirit!
    Thou can'st make the blind to see;
  Witnesser of Jesus' merit,
    Speak the word of power to me,—
      Even me, even me, etc.

5 Love of God, so pure and changeless;
    Blood of Christ, so rich and free;
  Grace of God, so strong and boundless,
    Magnify them all in me,—
      Even me, even me, etc.

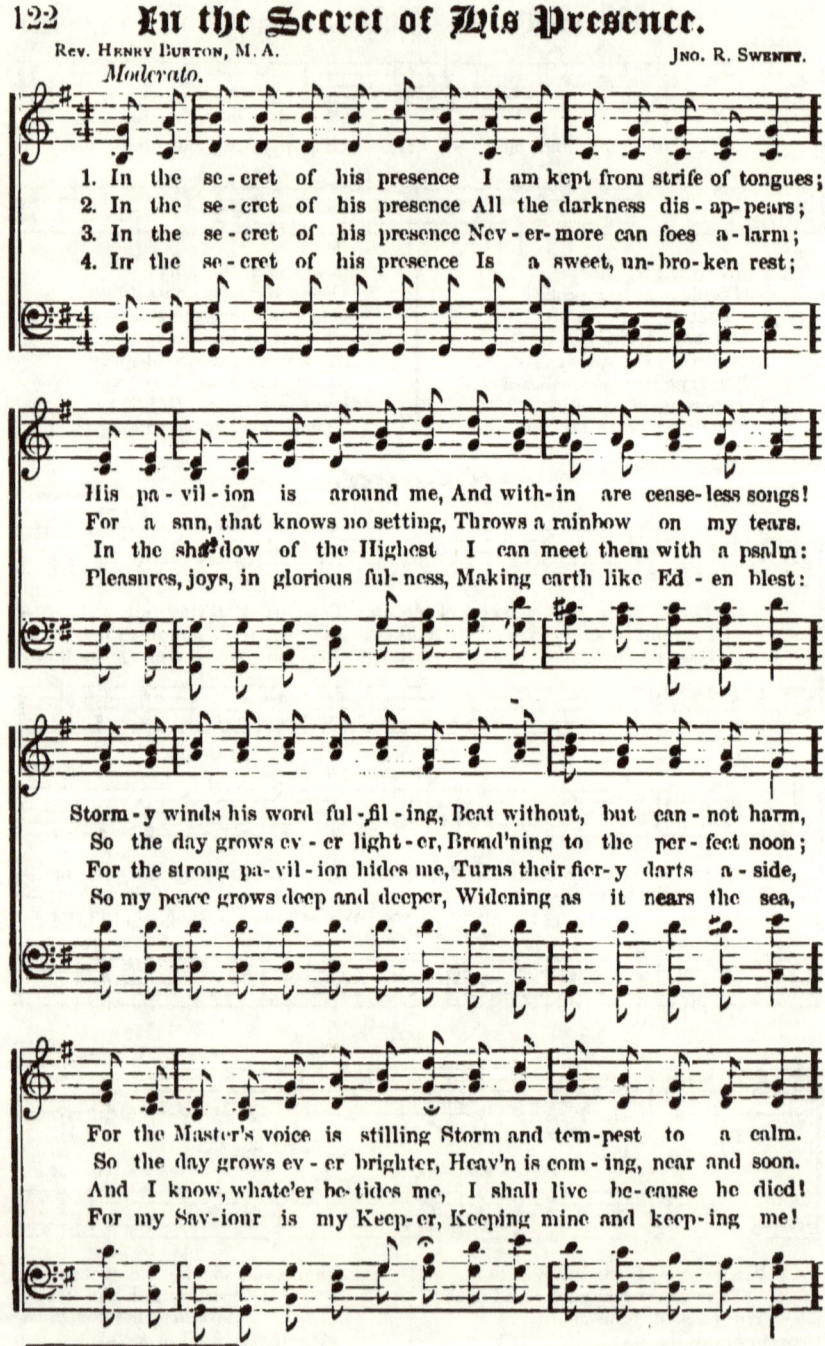

In the Secret of His Presence.—CONCL. 123

CHORUS.

In the se - - cret of his presence Jesus keeps, . . I know not how;
In the secret of his pres-ence   Jesus keeps, I know not how, I know not how;

In the sha - - dow of the High-est   I am resting, hiding now.
In the shadow of the Highest, In the shadow of the Highest,

Forever with the Lord.

JAMES MONTGOMERY.   Tune, VIGIL, S. M.

1. "For - ev - er with the Lord!"   A - men, so let it be!
2. Here in the bo - dy pent,   Ab - sent from him I roam,
3. "For - ev - er with the Lord!"   Fa - ther, if 'tis thy will,
4. So, when my lat - est breath   Shall rend the veil in twain,
5. Knowing as I am known,   How shall I love that word,

Life from the dead is in that word, 'Tis im - mor - tal - i - ty.
Yet night-ly pitch my mov-ing tent   A day's march nearer home.
The promise of that faithful word, E'en here to me ful - fil.
By death I shall es - cape from death, And life e - ter - nal gain.
And oft re-peat be - fore the throne, "Forev - er with the Lord!"

God Came Knocking.—CONCLUDED.

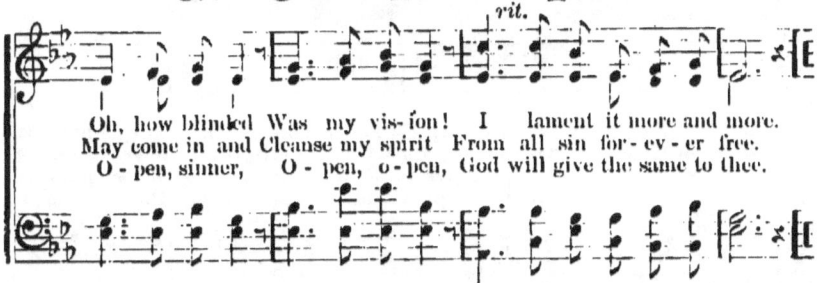

Oh, how blinded Was my vis-ion! I lament it more and more.
May come in and Cleanse my spirit From all sin for-ev-er free.
O-pen, sinner, O-pen, o-pen, God will give the same to thee.

I Dare Not Idle Stand.

"Look on the fields, for they are white already to harvest."—John iv. 35.

JOHN T. GRAPE.

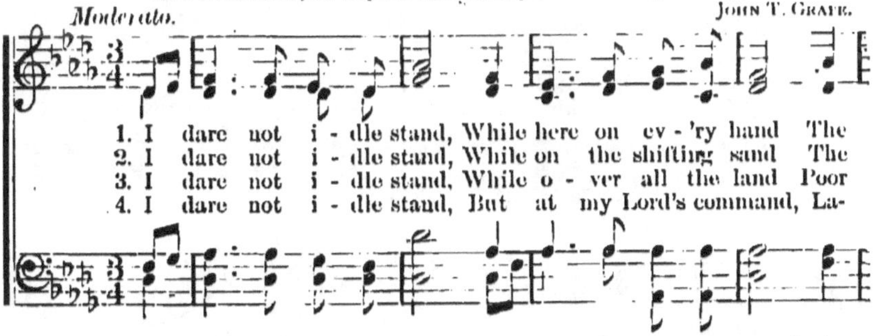

Moderato.

1. I dare not i-dle stand, While here on ev-'ry hand The
2. I dare not i-dle stand, While on the shifting sand The
3. I dare not i-dle stand, While o-ver all the land Poor
4. I dare not i-dle stand, But at my Lord's command, La-

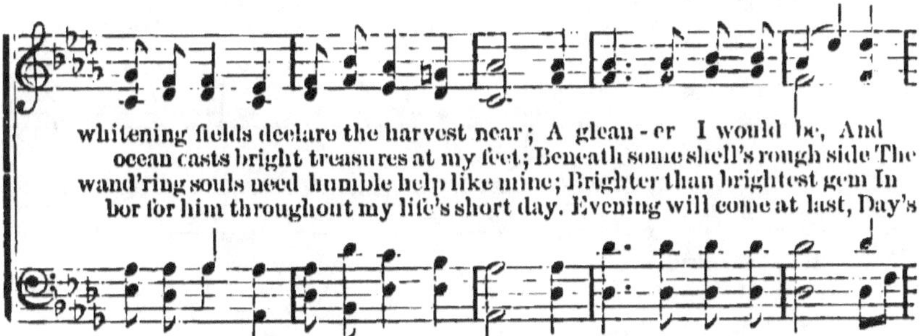

whitening fields declare the harvest near; A glean-er I would be, And
ocean casts bright treasures at my feet; Beneath some shell's rough side The
wand'ring souls need humble help like mine; Brighter than brightest gem In
bor for him throughout my life's short day. Evening will come at last, Day's

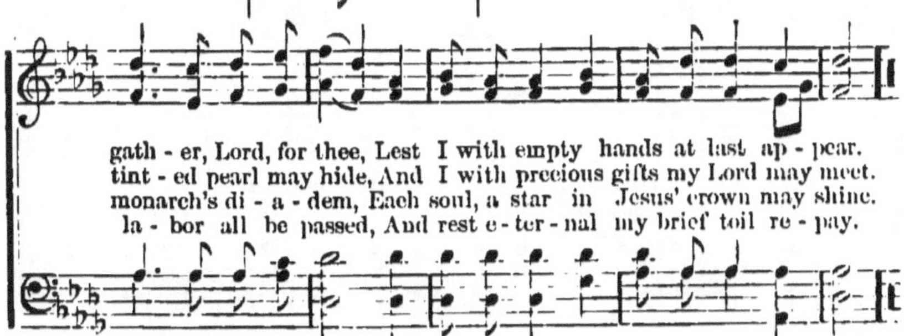

gath-er, Lord, for thee, Lest I with empty hands at last ap-pear.
tint-ed pearl may hide, And I with precious gifts my Lord may meet.
monarch's di-a-dem, Each soul, a star in Jesus' crown may shine.
la-bor all be passed, And rest e-ter-nal my brief toil re-pay.

From "Pearls of Gospel Song," by per.

128. Christ the Lord is King.

FANNY J. CROSBY. A. M. WORTMAN, M. D.

1. Shout for joy, ye ho-ly throng, Christ the Lord is King; An-gel harps, the sound prolong, Christ the Lord is King.
2. Shout for joy, ye nations all, Christ the Lord is King; Crowns before his throne shall fall, Christ the Lord is King.
3. He who rent the boasting grave, Christ the Lord, is King; He who lives the lost to save, Christ the Lord, is King.
4. Shout for joy, ye realms of night, Christ the Lord is King; Hail the beams of gospel light, Christ the Lord is King.

CHORUS.

Bear the news . . . from pole to pole, . . . Spread the truth . . . from sea to sea, . . .
Bear the news from pole to pole, Bear the news from pole to pole, Spread the truth from sea to sea, O, spread the truth from sea to sea,

Lo! the Prince . . . . of life and glo - - - - ry
Lo! the Prince of life and glo - ry, Lo! the Prince of life and glo - ry

King of heaven . . . . and earth shall be. . . . . .
King of heaven and earth shall be, and earth shall be.

Copyright, 1887, by John J. Hood.

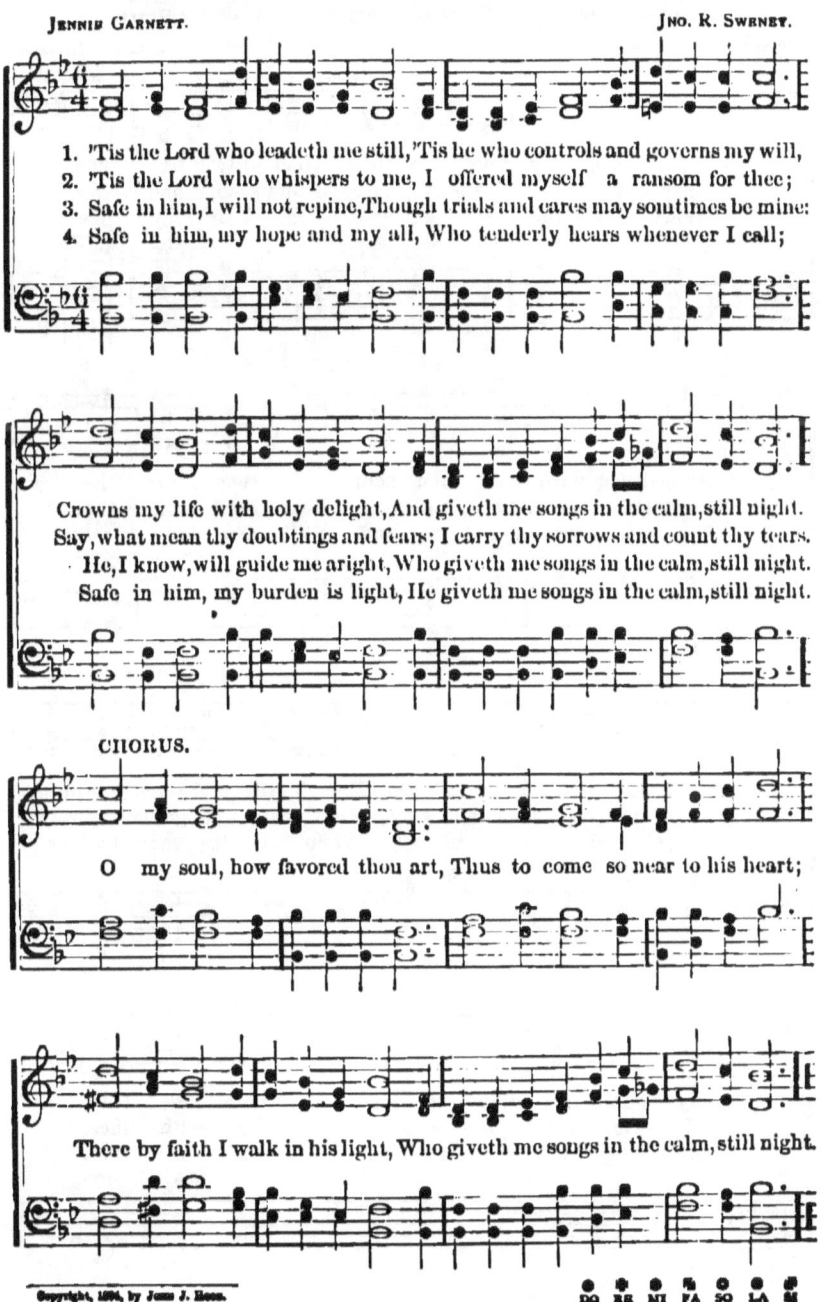

136. Stand at Your Post.

Lizzie Edwards.   Jno. R. Sweney.

1. Stand at your post, ye watchmen, Dark tho' the night; See afar, bright and clear,
2. Stand at your post of du-ty, Be not dismayed, Christ the Lord rideth on
3. Stand at your post of du-ty, Truth must prevail, Joyful news, welcome news,
4. Stand at your post of duty, Cheer, watchmen, cheer; Lo, the time, promised time,

Dawns the morning light; Sound, sound the trump of Zion O'er land and sea;
Now in strength arrayed; Lift up the gos-pel banner, Watchmen, proclaim
Comes with ev'ry gale; Lo! at the feet of Jesus Proud monarchs fall:
Now is drawing near; Bright o'er the distant mountain On rolls the day,

CHORUS.

Tell a-gain the happy tidings, Grace is free. Bright Star of the
Peace and life to ev-'ry creature Thro' his name.
They have heard the gospel message, Joy to all.
Driving ev-'ry mist and shadow Far a-way. Bright, bright Star,

morn - ing, Thou bles-sed Star of glo - ry, bles-sed Star of glo - ry,
bright, bright Star,

Copyright, 1886, by John J. Hood.

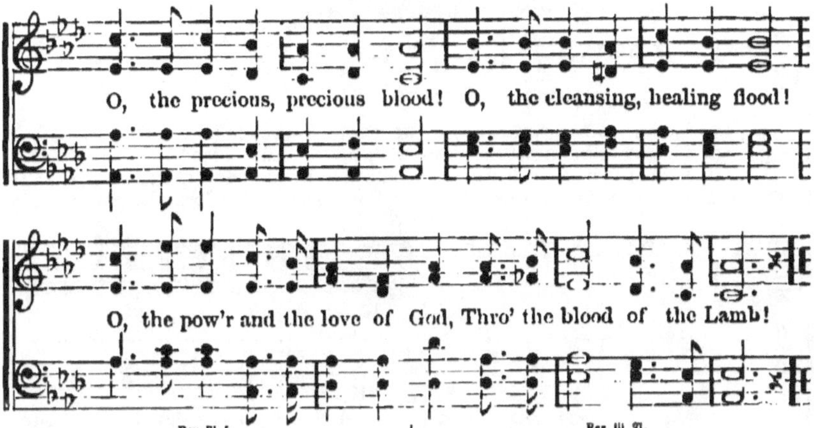

"Overcomers."—CONCLUDED.

O, the precious, precious blood! O, the cleansing, healing flood!

O, the pow'r and the love of God, Thro' the blood of the Lamb!

Rev. iii. 5.
5 ‖: What shall we hear? :‖ that over-
By the blood of the Lamb? [cometh
‖: He shall hear his name con-|fessed in heaven, :‖
That overcomes by the blood.

Rev. xxi. 7.
6 ‖: What shall he have? :‖ that over-
By the blood of the Lamb? [cometh
‖: God will give him all things, and| make him his son, :‖
That overcomes by the blood.

Rev. iii. 21.
7 ‖: Where shall he sit? :‖ that over-
By the blood of the Lamb? [cometh
‖: He shall sit with | Jesus, on his throne, :‖
That overcomes by the blood

1 John v. 4.
8 ‖: What is the victory? :‖ that over-
By the blood of the Lamb? [cometh
‖: Faith is the victory that | overcometh, ‖:
By the blood of the Lamb.

All the way long it is Jesus.

1. { O good old way, how sweet thou art! All the way long it is Je - sus;
   { May none of us from thee de-part; All the way long it is Je - sus.

CHORUS.
Je - sus, Je - sus, Why, all the way long it is Je - sus.

2 But may our actions always say
We're marching in the good old way.

3 This note above the rest shall swell,
That Jesus doeth all things well.

142. Trust in thy Deliverer.

LAURA MILLER.   JNO. R. SWENEY.

1. Go forth, O Christian sol-dier, Why shouldst thou fear to tread A path that bears the footprints Of him, thy living head; Take up thy cross with firm-ness, Whate'er that cross may be, Remember him who car-ried A great-er one for thee.

2. Be strong, O Christian sol-dier, And at thy post a-bide, Nor heed the arrows fall-ing From foes on ev-'ry side; Let nothing daunt thy cour-age, Whate'er the strife may be, But trust in thy Deliv-er-er, Who shed his blood for thee.

3. Stand fast, O Christian sol-dier, Nor lay thy ar-mor down Till thou by faith and patience Hast won the victor's crown; Then lift thy soul re-joic-ing, And let thy glo-ry be In him, the Great Deliv-er-er, Who shed his blood for thee.

CHORUS.

Trust in thy De-liv-er-er, Trust in thy De-liv-er-er, Oh, trust in thy De-liv-er-er, Who shed his blood for thee;

Copyright, 1876, by John J. Hood.

Trust in thy Deliverer.—CONCLUDED. 143

Oh, trust in thy De-liv-er-er, Who shed his blood for thee.

Shall we Meet Beyond the River?

H. L. HASTINGS.   ELISHA S. RICE.

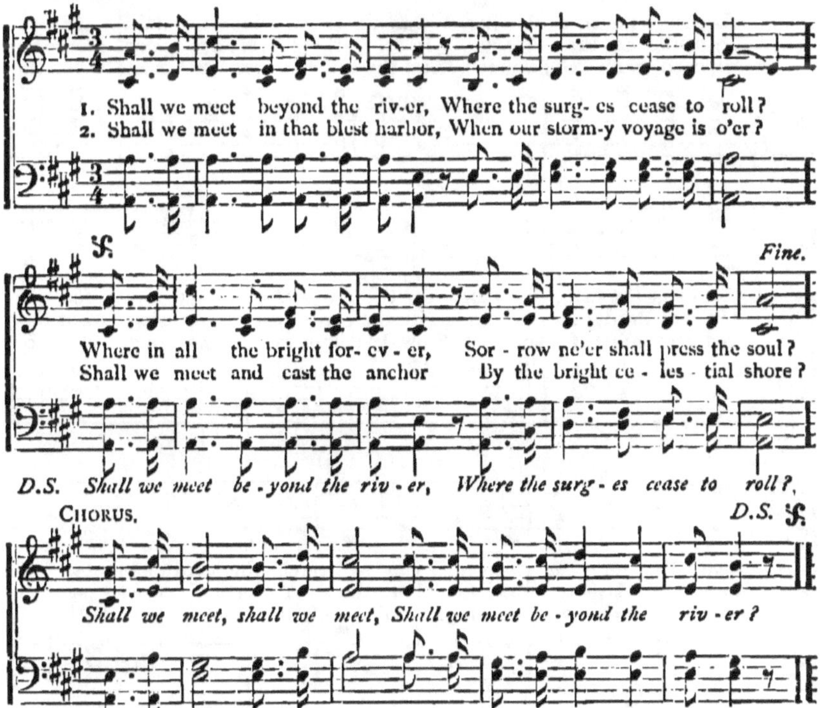

1. Shall we meet beyond the riv-er, Where the surg-es cease to roll?
2. Shall we meet in that blest harbor, When our storm-y voyage is o'er?

Where in all the bright for-ev-er, Sor-row ne'er shall press the soul?
Shall we meet and cast the anchor By the bright ce-les-tial shore?

D.S. Shall we meet be-yond the riv-er, Where the surg-es cease to roll?

CHORUS.   D.S.

Shall we meet, shall we meet, Shall we meet be-yond the riv-er?

3 Shall we meet in yonder city,
   Where the towers of crystal shine?
  Where the walls are all of jasper,
   Built by workmanship divine?

4 Where the music of the ransomed
   Rolls its harmony around,
  And creation swells the chorus
   With its sweet melodious sound?

5 Shall we meet there many a loved one,
   That was torn from our embrace?
  Shall we listen to their voices,
   And behold them face to face?

6 Shall we meet with Christ our Saviour,
   When he comes to claim his own?
  Shall we know his blessed favor,
   And sit down upon his throne?

From " New Silver Song," by permission.

When the Sheaves, etc.—CONCLUDED. 147

How shall we make answer For the talents given, When the sheaves are gathered in.

Glorious Fountain.

Cowper.   T. C. O'Kane.

1. { There is a fountain filled with blood, filled with blood, filled with blood, There
     And sinners plung'd beneath that flood, beneath that flood, beneath that flood, And
2. { The dy-ing thief rejoiced to see, rejoiced to see, rejoiced to see, The
     And there may I, tho' vile as he, tho' vile as he, tho' vile as he, And

is a fount-ain filled with bood, Drawn from Imman-uel's veins, }
sinners plunged beneath that flood, Lose all their guilt-y stains. }
dy-ing thief rejoiced to see That fount-ain in his day, }
there may I, tho' vile as he, Wash all my sins a-way. }

CHORUS.

Oh, glo-ri-ous fount-ain! Here will I stay, And in thee

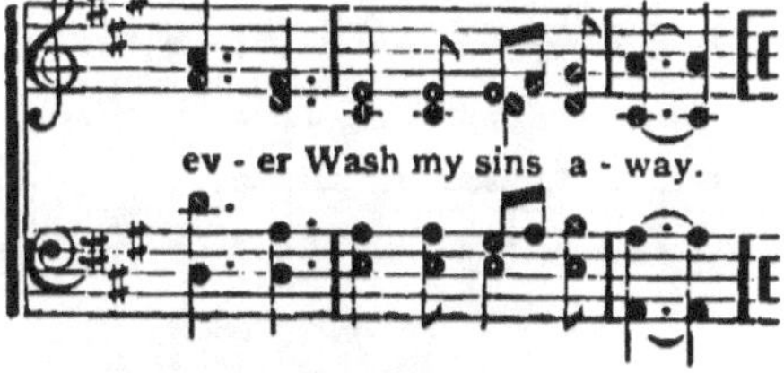

ev-er Wash my sins a-way.

3 Thou dying Lamb, ‖: thy precious blood :‖
  Shall never lose its power,
  Till all the ransomed ‖:Church of God :‖
  Are saved, to sin no more.

4 E'er since by faith ‖: I saw the stream :‖
  Thy flowing wounds supply,
  Redeeming love ‖: has been my theme,:‖
  And shall be till I die.

From "Redeemer's Praise," by per.

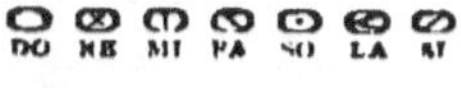

The Ark Floateth By.

Jno. R. Sweney.

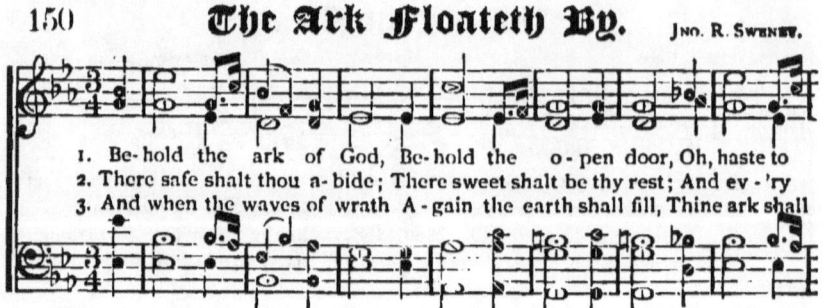

1. Be-hold the ark of God, Be-hold the o-pen door, Oh, haste to
2. There safe shalt thou a-bide; There sweet shalt be thy rest; And ev-'ry
3. And when the waves of wrath A-gain the earth shall fill, Thine ark shall

REFRAIN.

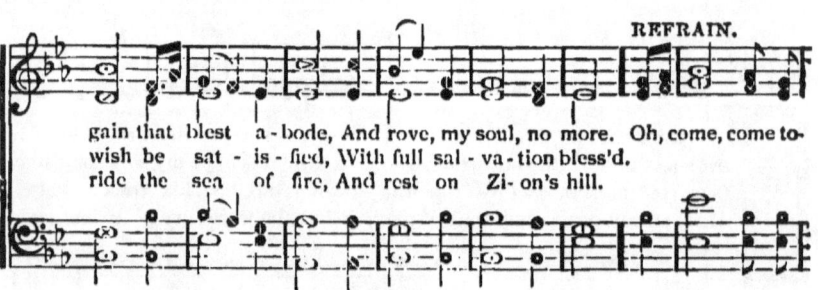

gain that blest a-bode, And rove, my soul, no more. Oh, come, come to-
wish be sat-is-fied, With full sal-va-tion bless'd.
ride the sea of fire, And rest on Zi-on's hill.

day, do not long-er de-lay, The ark, precious bark, floateth by; The

waves as they roll Shall not cover thy soul, For Jesus thy Saviour is nigh.

By permission.

Kneeling, Pleading, Waiting. 151

TATE & BRADY. "Peace through the blood of his cross."—Col. i. 26. E. A. HOFFMAN.

1. Have mer-cy, Lord, on me, As thou wert ev-er kind;
2. Blot out, O Lord, my sins, Nor me in an-ger view;
3. Withdraw not then thy help, Nor cast me from thy sight;
4. The joy thy fa-vor gives Let me a-gain ob-tain,

Let me, oppress'd with loads of guilt, Thy wonted mer-cy find.
Cre-ate in me a heart that's clean, An upright mind re-new.
Nor let thy Ho-ly Spir-it take His ev-er-last-ing flight.
And thy free Spir-it's firm support My fainting soul maintain.

CHORUS.

I am kneeling, at the cross, I am pleading, at the cross, I am kneeling, pleading, waiting to be saved; I am kneeling, at the cross, I am pleading, at the cross, There I'm kneeling, pleading, waiting to be saved.

Copyright, 1883, by JOHN J. HOOD.

DO RE MI FA SO LA SI

Have you not a Word for Jesus? 153

Frances R. Havergal. Warren W. Bentley.

1. Have you not a word for Jesus? Will you now his love proclaim?
2. He has spoken words of blessing, Pardon, peace and love to you,
3. Have you not a word for Jesus? Some perchance while you are dumb,
4. Yours may be the joy and honor Some poor ransomed soul to bring,

Refrain.—Have you not a word for Jesus? Will you now his love proclaim?

Fine.

Who will speak if you are silent, You who know and love his name?
Glorious hope and gracious comfort, Strong and tender, sweet and true;
Wait and weary for your message, Hoping you will bid them come;
Jewels for the coronation Of your coming Lord and King;

Who will speak if you are silent, You who know and love his name?

You whom he hath called and chosen His own witnesses to be,
Does he hear you telling others Something of his love untold,
Never telling hidden sorrows, Ling'ring just outside the door,
Will you cast away the gladness Thus your Master's joy to share,

D.C.

Will you tell your gracious Master, "Lord, we cannot speak for thee?"
Overflowings of thanksgiving, For his mercies manifold?
Longing for your hand to lead them Into rest forevermore.
All because a word for Jesus Seems too much for you to dare?

By permission.

DO RE MI FA SO LA SI

Follow the Lamb.

157

Rev. Wm. Hunter, D. D.　　　　　　　　　　　　Rev. J. H. Stockton.

1. O Jesus, immaculate Lamb! Thy faultless example I see,
And, conscious how feeble I am, For help look alone unto thee.

2. Thy word would I firmly believe, Thy footsteps unswerving pursue,
Thy spirit of meekness receive, Thy will with all diligence do.

CHORUS.
Oh, follow the Lamb! (spotless Lamb,) Follow the holy Lamb! (spotless Lamb,) To the living fountains he leads, Follow, oh, follow the Lamb!

3 Thy love in my heart shed abroad,
　A flame of pure loyalty there;
A zeal for the glory of God,
　Kept burning by watching and prayer.
　　Oh, follow the Lamb!

4 Thyself in my bosom enshrine,
　The Lord of my passions and will;
And all my new nature incline
　Thy law with delight to fulfil.
　　Oh, follow the Lamb!

5 No virtue of mine can I claim,
　No power to perform what I would;
The virtue is all in thy name,
　The power comes alone through thy [blood.
　　Oh, follow the Lamb!

6 Oh, save me completely from sin,
　Oh, wash me, and I shall be pure;
A thorough renewal within,
　A perfect and permanent cure.
　　Oh, follow the Lamb!

From "The Royal Fountain," by per.

All to Thee.

R. K. C.   R. Kelso Carter.

1. Je - sus, here I bring my all, Humbly at thy feet I fall,
2. Take my-self, my will, my choice, Means and talent, time and voice,
3. Lead me out to Ol - i - vet, On my brow the thorn-crown set,

In my soul re-solved to prove All that's in re-deeming love.
Loved ones, rep - u - tation's thrall, Present, fu - ture—take it all.
Lean - ing hard, my Lord, on thee, Let me die on Cal - va - ry!

CHORUS.

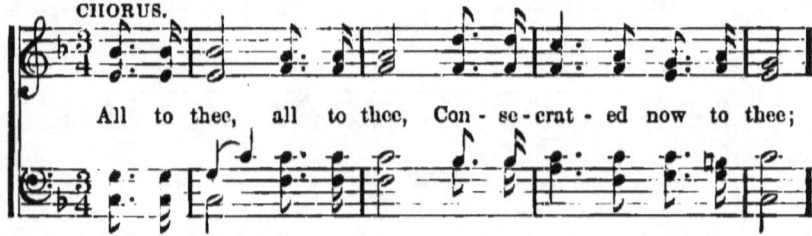

All to thee, all to thee, Con - se - crat - ed now to thee;

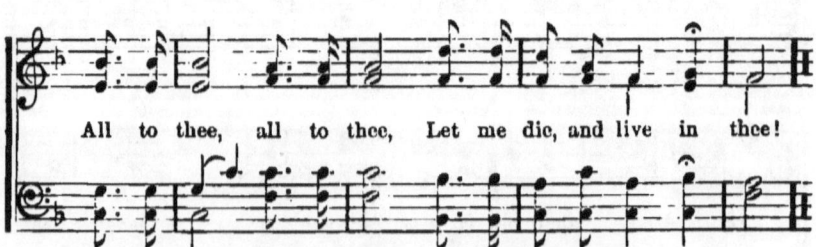

All to thee, all to thee, Let me die, and live in thee!

4 'Neath the judgment-thunders' boom
   Lay me in the silent tomb;
   Burst the bars, and, cleansed within,
   Raise me from the grave of sin.

5 Once for all, myself I give;
   Crucified, and yet I live;
   Yet not I, but Christ in me
   Lives and reigns eternally.

Copyright, 1886, by John J. Hood.

162. I'm more than Conqueror.

PARKER.   R. KELSO CARTER.

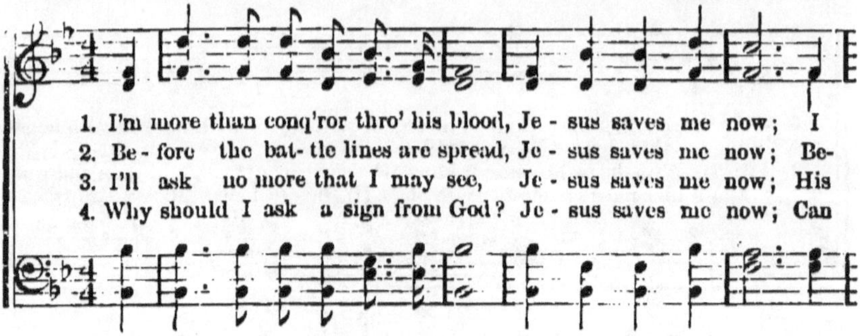

1. I'm more than conq'ror thro' his blood, Je-sus saves me now; I rest beneath the shield of God, Je-sus saves me now. I go a kingdom to ob-tain, I shall thro' him the vict'ry gain,— Je-sus saves me, Je-sus saves me now.
2. Be-fore the bat-tle lines are spread, Je-sus saves me now; Be-fore the boasting foe is dead, Je-sus saves me now. I win the fight tho' not be-gun, I'll trust and shout, still marching on,— Je-sus saves me, Je-sus saves me now.
3. I'll ask no more that I may see, Je-sus saves me now; His prom-ise is enough for me, Je-sus saves me now. Though foes be strong and walls be high, I'll shout, he gives the vic-to-ry,— Je-sus saves me, Je-sus saves me now.
4. Why should I ask a sign from God? Je-sus saves me now; Can I not trust the precious blood? Je-sus saves me now. Strong in his word, I meet the foe, And, shouting, win without a blow,— Je-sus saves me, Je-sus saves me now.

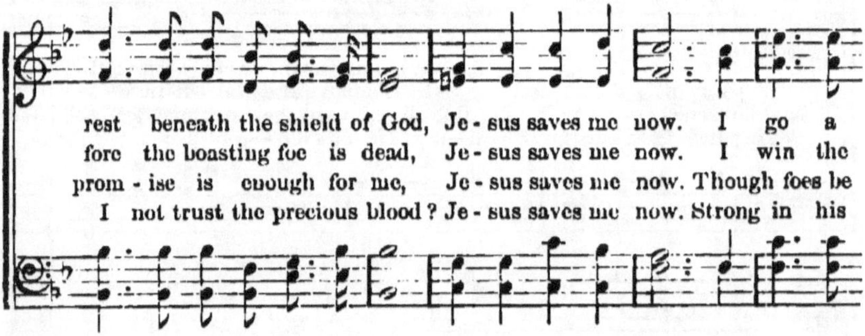

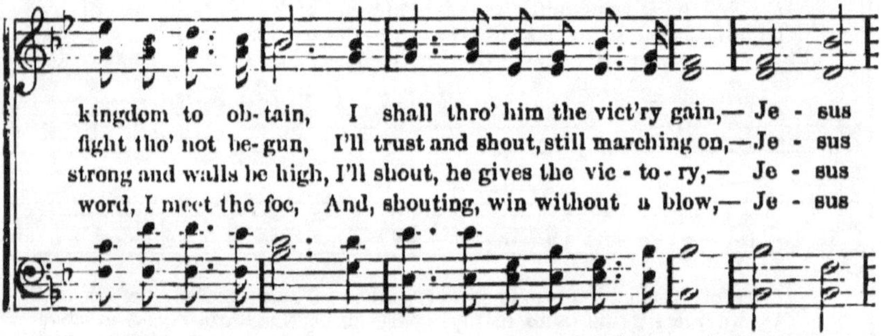

5 Should Satan come like 'whelming [waves,
   Jesus saves me now;
Ere trials crush my Father saves,
   Jesus saves me now.
He hides me till the storm is past
For me he tempers every blast,—
   Jesus saves me now.

Copyright, 1886, by JOHN J. HOOD.

The Cross and the Bible.—CONCLUDED. 167

lost ones of earth! O, the Cross .... and the Bi-ble for me.

From This Hour.

RACHEL ELLIOT. JNO R SWENEY.

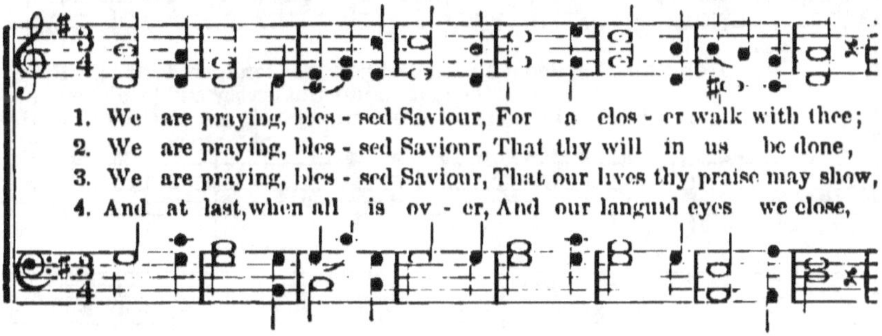

1. We are praying, bles-sed Saviour, For a clos-er walk with thee;
2. We are praying, bles-sed Saviour, That thy will in us be done,
3. We are praying, bles-sed Saviour, That our lives thy praise may show,
4. And at last, when all is ov-er, And our languid eyes we close,

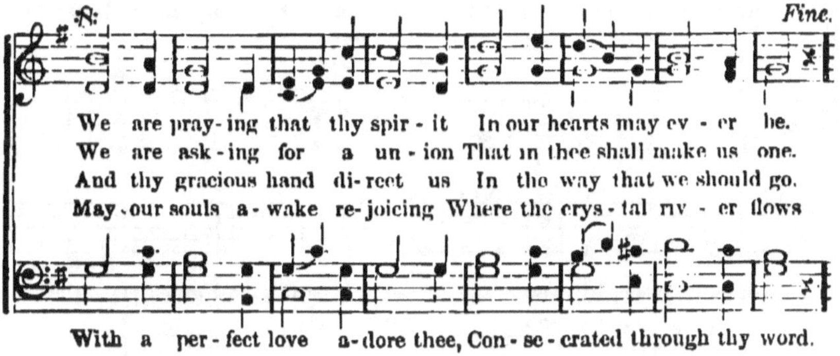

We are pray-ing that thy spir-it In our hearts may ev-er be.
We are ask-ing for a un-ion That in thee shall make us one.
And thy gracious hand di-rect us In the way that we should go.
May our souls a-wake re-joicing Where the crys-tal riv-er flows

With a per-fect love a-dore thee, Con-se-crated through thy word.

CHORUS.

From this hour, O gracious Lord, May each wak-ing heart be-fore thee

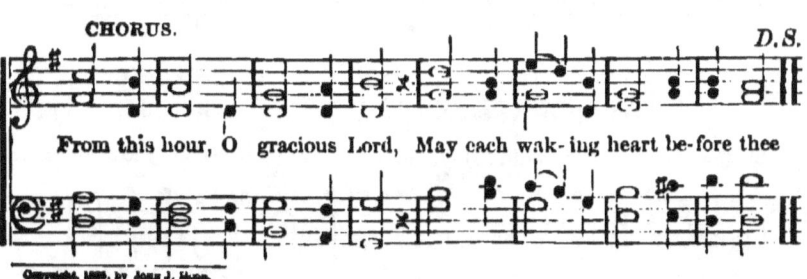

The New Song.—CONCLUDED.

3. Can my lips be mute, or my heart be sad,
When the gracious Master hath made me glad?
When he points where the many mansions be,
And sweetly says, 'There is one for thee'?

4. I shall catch the gleam of its jasper wall
When I come to the gloom of the evenfall,
For I know that the shadows, dreary and dim,
Have a path of light that will lead to him.

From "Gems of Praise," by per.

Fill Me Now.

Rev. E. H. Stokes, D.D.   Jno. R. Sweney.

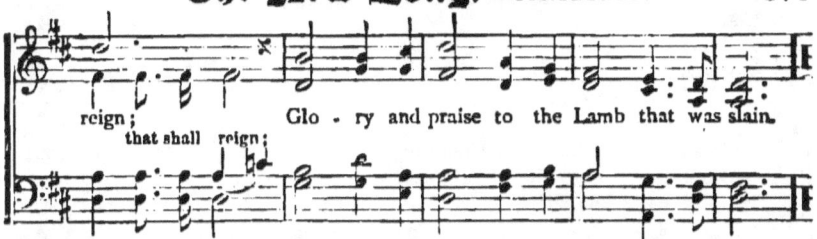

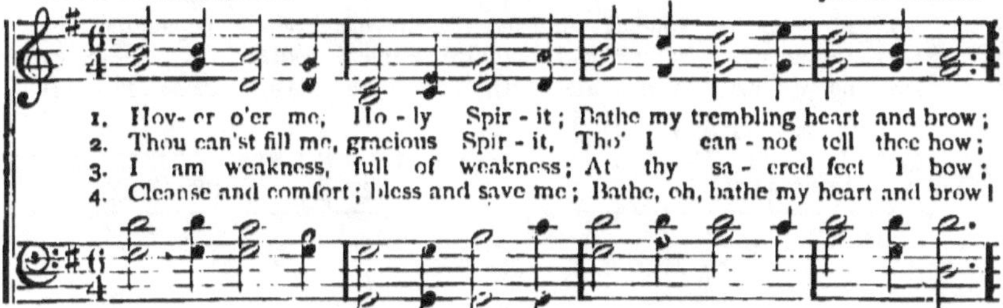

1. Hov-er o'er me, Ho-ly Spir-it; Bathe my trembling heart and brow;
2. Thou can'st fill me, gracious Spir-it, Tho' I can-not tell thee how;
3. I am weakness, full of weakness; At thy sa-cred feet I bow;
4. Cleanse and comfort; bless and save me; Bathe, oh, bathe my heart and brow!

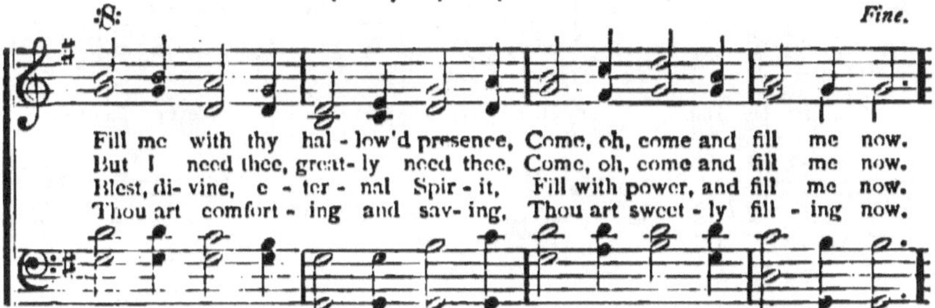

Fill me with thy hal-low'd presence, Come, oh, come and fill me now.
But I need thee, great-ly need thee, Come, oh, come and fill me now.
Blest, di-vine, e-ter-nal Spir-it, Fill with power, and fill me now.
Thou art comfort-ing and sav-ing, Thou art sweet-ly fill-ing now.

D.S. Fill me with thy hal-low'd presence,—Come, oh, come and fill me now.

CHORUS.   **D.S.**

Fill me now, fill me now, Je-sus, come, and fill me now;

Copyright, 1879, by John J. Hood.

Are You Washed in the Blood. 175

E. A. H.
Rev. E. A. Hoffman.

1. Have you been to Jesus for the cleansing power? Are you washed in the blood of the Lamb? Are you fully trusting in his grace this hour? Are you washed in the blood of the Lamb?
2. Are you walking daily by the Saviour's side? Are you washed in the blood of the Lamb? Do you rest each moment in the Crucified? Are you washed in the blood of the Lamb?
3. When the Bridegroom cometh, will your robes be white, Pure and white in the blood of the Lamb? Will your soul be ready for the mansions bright, And be washed in the blood of the Lamb?
4. Lay aside the garments that are stained with sin, And be washed in the blood of the Lamb? There's a fountain flowing for the soul unclean, O be washed in the blood of the Lamb!

CHORUS.

Are you washed in the blood, In the soul-cleansing blood of the Lamb? Are your garments spotless? Are they white as snow? Are you washed in the blood of the Lamb?

By permission.

Until Ye Find.—CONCLUDED.

miss - ing one must not be lost,—Go, seek un - til ye find.
miss - ing one, no long - er lost, The miss-ing one is found.

4 I've sought my friends for many a day,
  Have prayed for many a year;
  Yet, still they wander far away,
  O'er mountains dark and drear;
  How long thus seek with burdened mind?
  "Seek," Jesus saith, "until ye find;"
  The missing one must not be lost,—
  "Go, seek until ye find!"

5 Lord, at thy word I go again,
  Believing I shall find:
  I listened, and a low refrain
  Came to me on the wind;
  Led by the sadly joyful sound
  I rushed, and, lo, the lost was found!
  Joy! joy! O blessed joy divine!
  The lost one I have found.

Trustingly.

H. BONAR. Wm. J. KIRKPATRICK.

1. Trust - ing - ly, trust - ing - ly, Je - sus, to thee Come I; Lord,
2. Peace - ful - ly, peace - ful - ly Walk I with thee; Je - sus, my
3. Hap - pi - ly, hap - pi - ly Pass I a - long, Ea - ger to

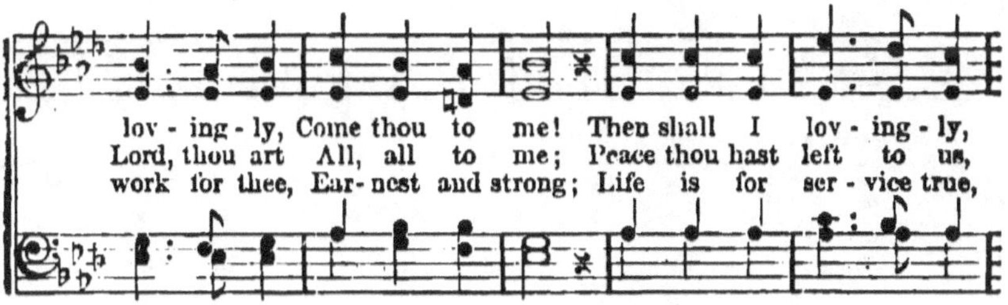

lov - ing - ly, Come thou to me! Then shall I lov - ing - ly,
Lord, thou art All, all to me; Peace thou hast left to us,
work for thee, Ear - nest and strong; Life is for ser - vice true,

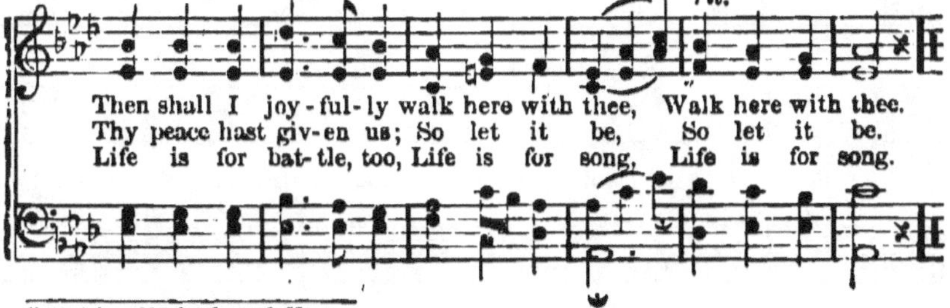

rit.

Then shall I joy - ful - ly walk here with thee, Walk here with thee.
Thy peace hast giv - en us; So let it be, So let it be.
Life is for bat - tle, too, Life is for song, Life is for song.

Copyright, 1885, by JOHN J. HOOD.

The Song of the Soul.

Rev. Henry A. von Dulsem. T. C. O'Kane.

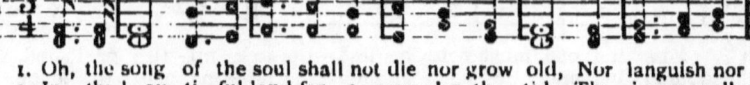

1. Oh, the song of the soul shall not die nor grow old, Nor languish nor
2. In the beau-ti-ful land far a-way o'er the tide, The jasper-walled
3. And the fair, golden harps in the hands of the blest, Shall thrill to a
4. And as a-ges fly onward, tho' worlds cease to be, And per-ish the

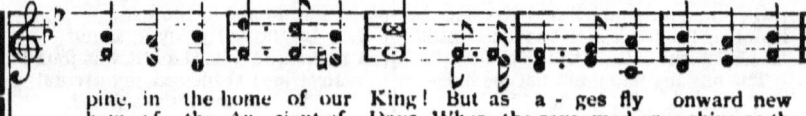

pine, in the home of our King! But as a-ges fly onward new
home of the An-cient of Days, Where the ransomed ones shine as the
touch that no an-gel can give, As we sing in that land where the
stars that in heav-en do throng, Still the joy of the soul shall be

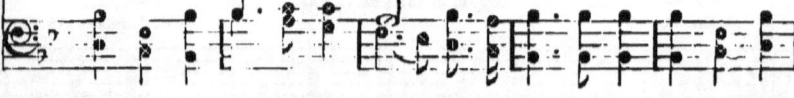

chords shall un-fold, New mel-o-dies meeting, in-spire us to sing.
sun in his pride, Our long hal-le-lu-jahs of glo-ry we'll raise.
wea-ry shall rest, Of One who hath died that a sin-ner might live.
deathless and free, And deathless and free the sweet notes of her song.

REFRAIN.

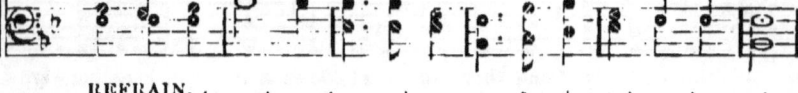

Oh, the song of the soul! Oh, the song of the soul!

For-ev-er in glo-ry the song of the soul!

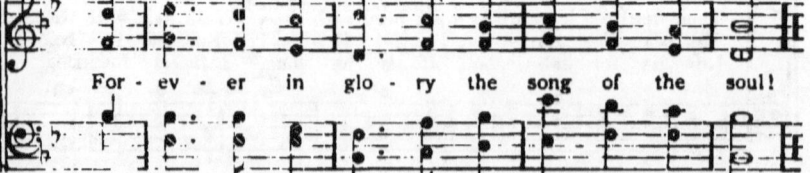

From "Redeemer's Praise," by per.

The Great Physician.

Rev Wm. H. Hunter, D. D. Arranged by J. H. Stockton.

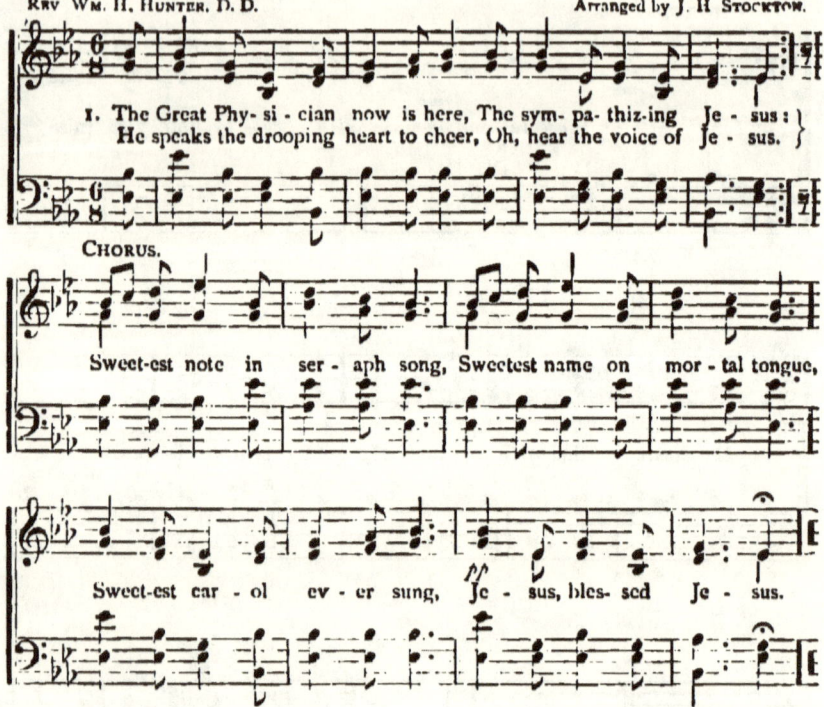

1. The Great Phy-si-cian now is here, The sym-pa-thiz-ing Je-sus;
He speaks the drooping heart to cheer, Oh, hear the voice of Je-sus.

CHORUS.
Sweet-est note in ser-aph song, Sweetest name on mor-tal tongue,
Sweet-est car-ol ev-er sung, Je-sus, bles-sed Je-sus.

2 Your many sins are all forgiven,
  Oh, hear the voice of Jesus;
Go on your way in peace to heaven,
  And wear a crown with Jesus.

3 All glory to the dying Lamb!
  I now believe in Jesus;
I love the blessed Saviour's name,
  I love the name of Jesus.

4 The children too, both great and small,
  Who love the name of Jesus,
May now accept his gracious call
  To work and live for Jesus.

5 Come, brethren, help me sing his praise,
  Oh, praise the name of Jesus;
Come, sisters, all your voices raise,
  Oh, bless the name of Jesus.

6 His name dispels my guilt and fear,
  No other name but Jesus;
Oh, how my soul delights to hear
  The precious name of Jesus.

7 And when to that bright world above,
  We rise to see our Jesus,
We'll sing around the throne of love
  His name, the name of Jesus.

MY SOUL, BE ON THY GUARD. — Laban, key D.

1 My soul, be on thy guard,
    Ten thousand foes arise;
  The hosts of sin are pressing hard
    To draw thee from the skies.

2 Oh, watch, and fight, and pray;
    The battle ne'er give o'er;
  Renew it boldly every day,
    And help divine implore.

3 Ne'er think the vict'ry won,
    Nor lay thine armor down;
  The work of faith will not be done
    Till thou obtain the crown.

4 Then persevere till death
    Shall bring thee to thy God;
  He'll take thee, at thy parting breath,
    To his divine abode.

Yield not to Temptation.

H. R. PALMER. By per.

1. Yield not to tempta-tion, For yielding is sin, Each vict'ry will help you
2. Shun e-vil companions, Bad language disdain, God's name hold in rev'rence,
3. To him that o'ercometh God giveth a crown, Thro' faith we will conquer,

some oth-er to win; Fight manfully onward, Dark passions sub- due,
nor take it in vain; Be thoughtful and earnest, Kind-hearted and true,
though often cast down; He who is our Saviour, Our strength will renew,

CHORUS.

Look ev-er to Je-sus, He'll car-ry you through. Ask the Saviour to help you,

Comfort, strengthen, and keep you, He is willing to aid you, He will carry you through.

STAND UP FOR JESUS.—*Webb, key B flat.*

1 Stand up! stand up for Jesus!
 Ye soldiers of the cross;
 Lift high his royal banner,
 It must not suffer loss;
 From victory unto victory
 His army he shall lead,
 Till every foe is vanquished,
 And Christ is Lord indeed.

2 Stand up! stand up for Jesus!
 Stand in his strength alone;
 The arm of flesh will fail you,—
 Ye dare not trust your own;

Put on the gospel armor,
 And, watching unto prayer,
 Where duty calls, or danger,
 Be never wanting there.

3 Stand up! stand up for Jesus!
 The strife will not be long;
 This day the noise of battle,
 The next the victor's song;
 To him that overcometh
 A crown of life shall be,
 He with the King of Glory
 Shall reign eternally.

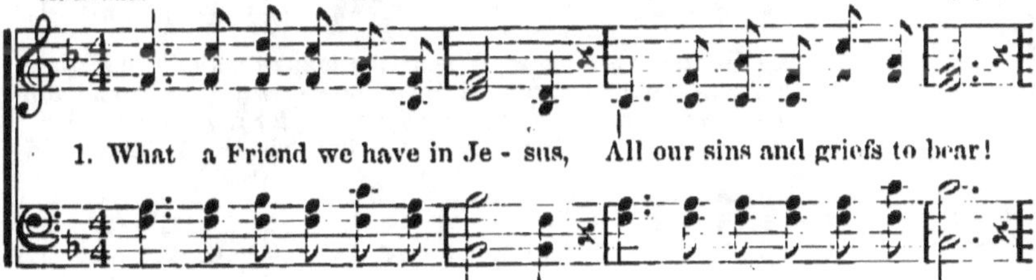

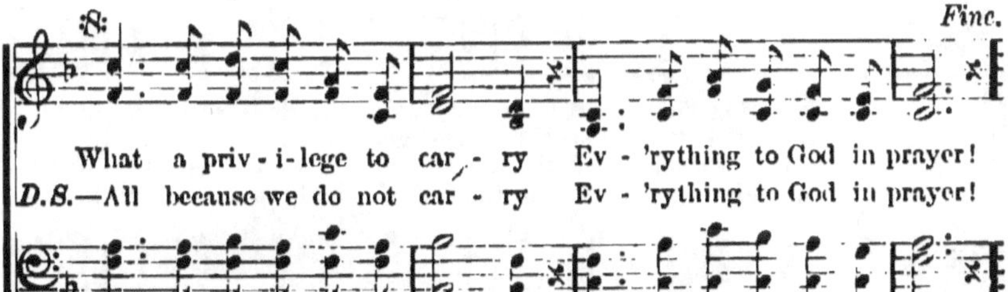

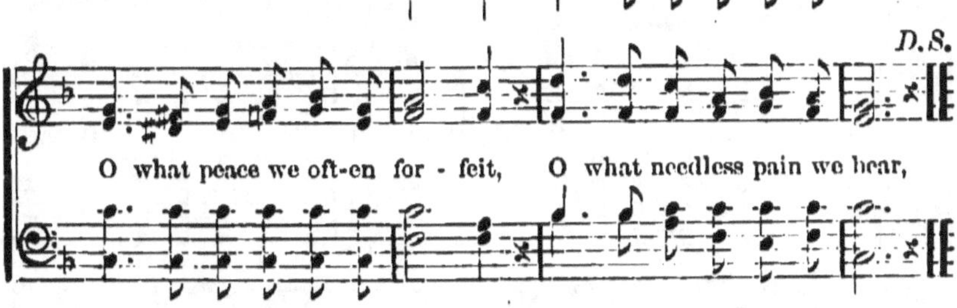

2 Have we trials and temptations?
  Is there trouble anywhere?
We should never be discouraged,
  Take it to the Lord in prayer.
Can we find a friend so faithful
  Who will all our sorrows share?
Jesus knows our every weakness,
  Take it to the Lord in prayer.

3 Are we weak and heavy laden,
  Cumbered with a load of care?—
Precious Saviour, still our refuge,—
  Take it to the Lord in prayer.
Do thy friends despise, forsake thee?
  Take it to the Lord in prayer;
In his arms he'll take and shield thee,
  Thou wilt find a solace there.

rap - turous sight Of the beau - tiful glory-crowned hills. beautiful hills.

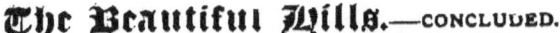

Eternity!—Where?

A young man was working alone in a large room in which was a big clock, the loud ticking of which seemed to frame itself into the words, "Eternity!—where?" Unable to endure any longer the reflections thus awakened, he arose and stopped the clock; but the question, "Eternity!—where?" still so haunted him, that he threw down his work, and hurrying home, determined that he would not allow anything to engage his thoughts till he could satisfactorily answer that searching question, "Eternity!—where?"

JNO. R. SWENEY.

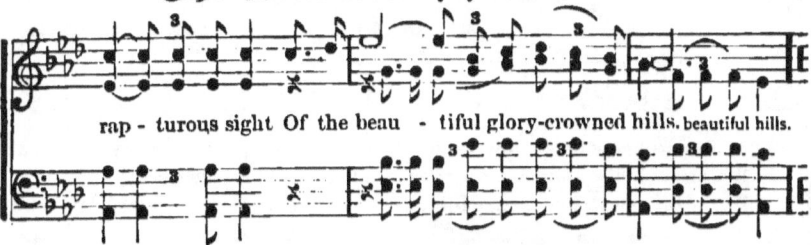

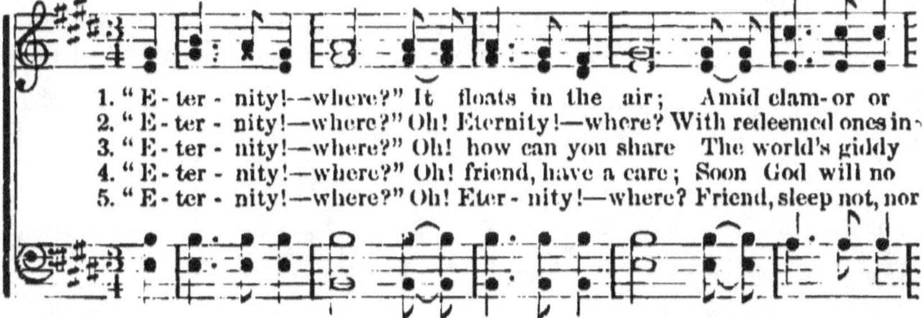
1. "E - ter - nity!—where?" It floats in the air; Amid clam - or or
2. "E - ter - nity!—where?" Oh! Eternity!—where? With redeemed ones in
3. "E - ter - nity!—where?" Oh! how can you share The world's giddy
4. "E - ter - nity!—where?" Oh! friend, have a care; Soon God will no
5. "E - ter - nity!—where?" Oh! Eter - nity!—where? Friend, sleep not, nor

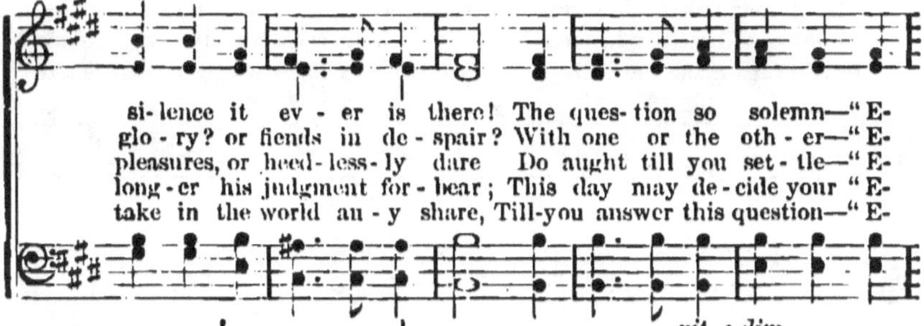
si - lence it ev - er is there! The ques - tion so solemn—"E-
glo - ry? or fiends in de - spair? With one or the oth - er—"E-
pleasures, or heed - less - ly dare Do aught till you set - tle—"E-
long - er his judgment for - bear; This day may de - cide your "E-
take in the world an - y share, Till-you answer this question—"E-

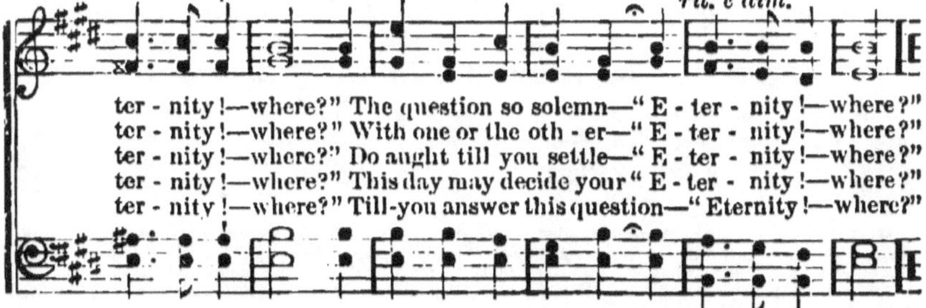
rit. e dim.
ter - nity!—where?" The question so solemn—"E - ter - nity!—where?"
ter - nity!—where?" With one or the oth - er—"E - ter - nity!—where?"
ter - nity!—where?" Do aught till you settle—"E - ter - nity!—where?"
ter - nity!—where?" This day may decide your "E - ter - nity!—where?"
ter - nity!—where?" Till-you answer this question—"Eternity!—where?"

DO RE MI FA SO LA SI

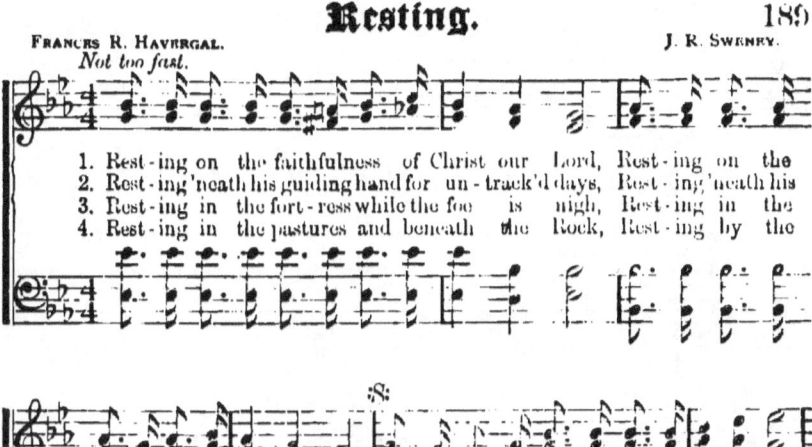

Pleading with thee.—CONCLUDED.

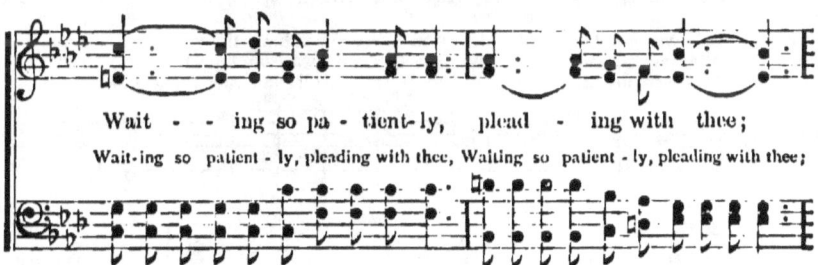

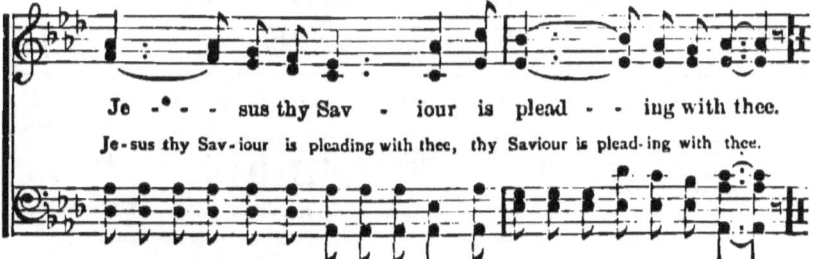

194. It is Good to be Here.

Rev. I. N. Wilson. Jno R. Sweney, by per.

1. While we bow in thy name, Oh, meet us again, Fill our hearts with the light of thy love;
May the Spirit of grace, And the smiles of thy face, Gently fall on us now from above.

REFRAIN.
It is good to be here, it is good to be here, Thy perfect love now drives away all our fear, And light streaming down makes the pathway all clear, It is good for us, Lord, to be here.

2 Our souls long for thee;
  Oh, may we now see
A sin-cleansing blood-wave appear;
  And feel, as it rolls
  In power o'er our souls,
It is good for us, Lord, to be here.

3 Thou art with us, we know;
  We feel the sweet flow [tide;
Of the sin-cleansing wave's gladd'ning
  We are washed from our sin,
  Made all holy within,
And in Jesus we sweetly abide.

Copyright, 1879, by Jno. R. Sweney.

OH, HOW HAPPY ARE THEY.   Tune and Chorus above.

Oh, how happy are they
  Who the Saviour obey,
And have laid up their treasures above;
  Tongue can never express
  The sweet comfort and peace
Of a soul in its earliest love.

2 That sweet comfort was mine,
  When the favor divine
I received thro' the blood of the Lamb;
  When my heart first believed,
  What a joy I received—
What a heaven in Jesus' name!

3 'Twas a heaven below
  My Redeemer to know,
And the angels could do nothing more
  Than to fall at his feet,
  And the story repeat,
And the Lover of sinners adore.

4 Jesus, all the day long,
  Was my joy and my song;
Oh, that all his salvation might see:
  He hath loved me, I cried,
  He hath suffered and died,
To redeem even rebels like me.

I am Thinking of Home.

1. I am thinking of home, of my Father's house, Where the many bright mansions be!
2. I am thinking of home, of the lov'd ones there, Dearest friends who have gone before;
3. I am thinking of home, yes, of home, sweet home; May we all in that home unite

Of the city whose streets are all covered with gold, Of its jasper walls pure and
With whom we went down to the death-river's side, And so sadly thought as we
With the white-covered throng, and exultingly raise To the triune God, sweetest

fair to be-hold, Which the righteous a-lone ev-er see.
watched by the tide, Of the thrice hap-py morn-ings of yore.
an-thems of praise, Sing-ing, Glo-ry, and hon-or, and might.

REFRAIN.

O, home, sweet home, sweet home, I am thinking and longing for home; Beyond the pearly gates many mansions wait For the weary ones who journey home.

Homeward Bound.

1 OUT on an ocean all boundless we ride,
  We're homeward bound,
Tossed on the waves of a rough restless tide,
  We're homeward bound;
Far from the safe, quiet harbor we've rode,
Seeking our Father's celestial abode,
Promise of which on us each he bestowed,
  We're homeward bound.

2 Wildly the storm sweeps us on as it roars,
  We're homeward bound;
Look! yonder lie the bright heavenly shores,
  We're homeward bound;
Steady, O pilot! stand firm at the wheel,
Steady! we soon shall outweather the gale,
Oh, how we fly 'neath the loud-creaking sail
  We're homeward bound.

3 Into the harbor of heaven now we glide,
  We're home at last;
Softly we drift on its bright silver tide,
  We're home at last;
Glory to God! all our dangers are o'er,
We stand secure on the glorified shore,
Glory to God! we will shout evermore,
  We're home at last.

196. I shall have Wings.

On the steam ferry-boat plying between Liverpool and Birkenhead there might have been seen a few years ago a poor crippled boy, his body was grown almost to a man's size, but his limbs were withered and helpless, and not bigger than the limbs of a child. He used to wheel himself about in a small carriage. He had a little musical instrument on which he played, and while he never asked for anything, very few of the passengers could hear his sweet music, or look at his honest, cheerful face, without dropping a penny or two into his carriage. One day a lady was standing near, looking at him with great pity; she thought how sad and lonely he must feel, unable to help himself, and with no prospect of ever being any better in this world, and turning to a friend who was with her, she said, "poor boy, what a sad life he has to lead, and nothing in all the future to look forward too." She did not intend that he should hear this remark, but he did hear it, and as she was leaving the boat she saw a tear in his eye, and a bright smile on his face trying to chase the tear away, as he said, "I'm expecting to have wings some day, lady."

FANNY J. CROSBY.   JNO. R. SWENEY.

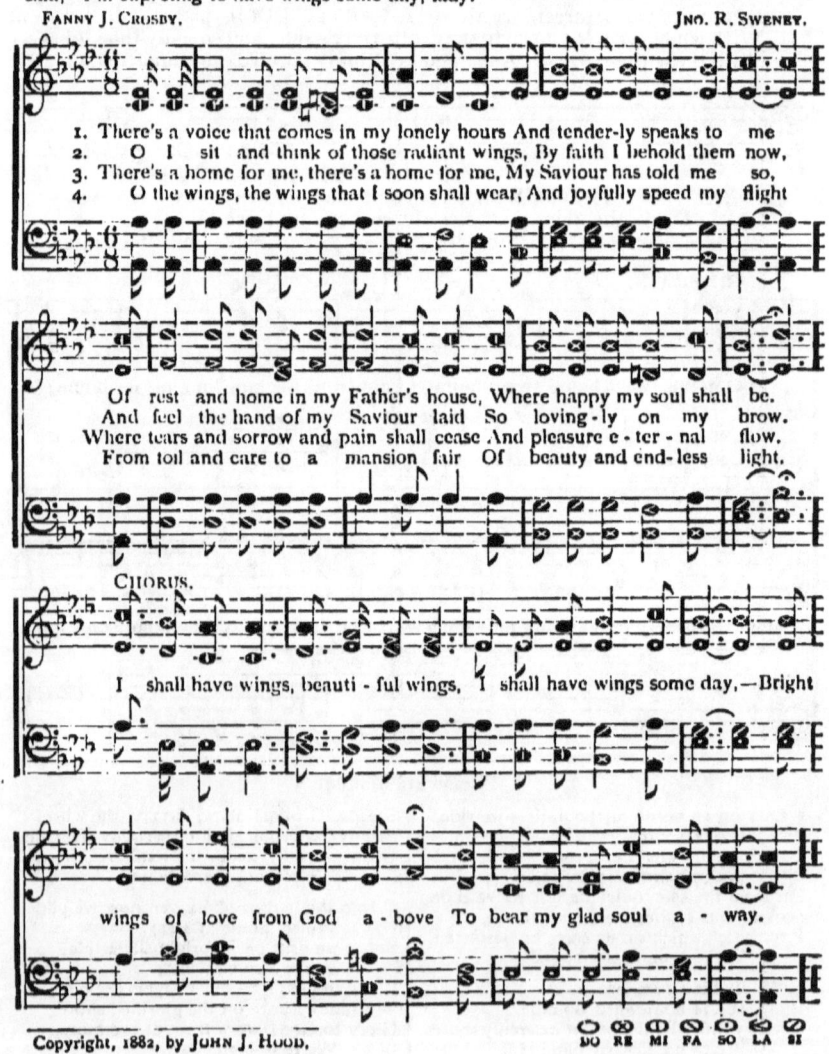

1. There's a voice that comes in my lonely hours And tender-ly speaks to me
2. O I sit and think of those radiant wings, By faith I behold them now,
3. There's a home for me, there's a home for me, My Saviour has told me so,
4. O the wings, the wings that I soon shall wear, And joyfully speed my flight

Of rest and home in my Father's house, Where happy my soul shall be.
And feel the hand of my Saviour laid So loving-ly on my brow.
Where tears and sorrow and pain shall cease And pleasure e - ter - nal flow.
From toil and care to a mansion fair Of beauty and end-less light.

CHORUS.

I shall have wings, beauti - ful wings, I shall have wings some day,—Bright wings of love from God a - bove To bear my glad soul a - way.

Copyright, 1882, by JOHN J. HOOD.

DO RE MI FA SO LA SI

Saw ye my Saviour?
SCOTCH MELODY.

died on Calvary, To atone for you and me, And to purchase our pardon with blood.

2 He was extended, he was extended,
  Painfully nailed to the cross;
                    to the cross;
  Here he bowed his head and died;
  Thus my Lord was crucified
  To atone for a world that was lost.

3 Hail, mighty Saviour! hail, mighty Saviour!
  Prince, and the Author of peace!
            the Author of peace!
  Oh! he bursts the bars of death!
  And, triumphant from the earth,
  He ascended to the mansions of bliss.

4 There interceding, there interceding,
  Pleading that sinners may live;
                that sinners may live;
  Crying, "Father, I have died;
  Oh, behold my hands and side!
  Oh, forgive them! I pray thee forgive!"

5 "I will forgive them, I will forgive them
  When they repent and believe;
                    and believe;
  Let them now return to thee,
  And be reconciled to thee,
  And salvation they all shall receive."

Saw ye my Saviour?
To my friend J. R. Sweney.   Wm. G. Fischer.

Copyright, 1880, by John J. Hood.

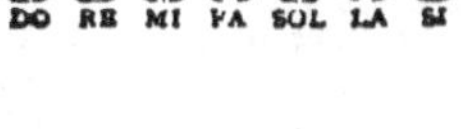

DO RE MI FA SOL LA SI

Jesus Paid it All.

Mrs. Elvina M. Hall.   John T. Grape. By per.

1. I hear the Sav-iour say, Thy strength in-deed is small;
Child of weakness, watch and pray, Find in me thine all in all.

CHORUS.
Je-sus paid it all, All to him I owe;
Sin had left a crim-son stain, He wash'd it white as snow.

2 Lord, now indeed I find
   Thy power, and thine alone,
   Can change the leper's spots,
   And melt the heart of stone.
    Jesus paid it all, etc.

3 For nothing good have I
   Whereby thy grace to claim,—
   I'll wash my garment white
   In the blood of Calvary's Lamb.
    Jesus paid it all, etc.

4 When from my dying bed
   My ransomed soul shall rise,
   Then " Jesus paid it all "
   Shall rend the vaulted skies.
    Jesus paid it all, etc.

5 And when before the throne
   I stand in him complete,
   I'll lay my trophies down,
   All down at Jesus' feet.
    Jesus paid it all, etc.

Only Trust Him.—CONCLUDED.

Only trust him now; He will save you, he will save you, He will save you now.
Come to Jesus now;

205 **Jesus is Mine!**

"My beloved is mine."—S of Sol. ii. 16.

Mrs. CATHARINE J. BONAR. T. E. PERKINS. By per.

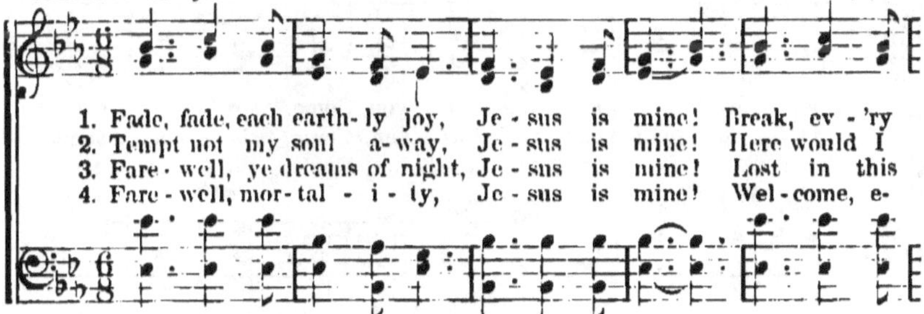

1. Fade, fade, each earth-ly joy, Jesus is mine! Break, ev-'ry ten-der tie, Jesus is mine! Dark is the wil-derness,
2. Tempt not my soul a-way, Jesus is mine! Here would I ev-er stay, Jesus is mine! Per-ish-ing things of clay,
3. Fare-well, ye dreams of night, Jesus is mine! Lost in this dawn-ing light, Jesus is mine! All that my soul has tried
4. Fare-well, mor-tal-i-ty, Jesus is mine! Wel-come, e-ter-ni-ty, Jesus is mine! Wel-come, O loved and blest,

Earth has no resting place, Jesus alone can bless, Jesus is mine!
Born but for one brief day, Pass from my heart away, Jesus is mine!
Left but a dismal void, Jesus has sat-is-fied, Jesus is mine!
Welcome, sweet scenes of rest, Welcome, my Saviour's breast, Jesus is mine!

208. The Child of a King.

1 My Father is rich in houses and lands,
He holdeth the wealth of the world in his hands!
Of rubies and diamonds, of silver and gold
His coffers are full,—he has riches untold.
Cho.—I'm the child of a King,
The child of a King;
With Jesus my Saviour
I'm the child of a King.

2 My Father's own Son, who saves us from sin, [men,
Once wandered o'er earth as the poorest of But now he is reigning forever on high,
And will give me a home in heaven by and by.

3 I once was an outcast stranger on earth,
A sinner by choice, an alien by birth!
But I've been adopted, my name's written down,—
An heir to a mansion, a robe, and a crown.

4 A tent or a cottage, why should I care?
They're building a palace for me over there! [sing:
Though exiled from home, yet still I may
All glory to God, I'm the child of a King.

209. The Solid Rock.

E. MOTE.   WM. B. BRADBURY.

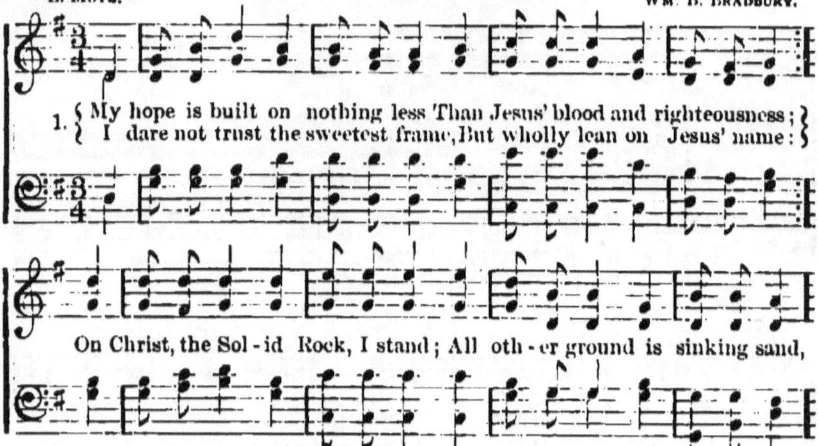

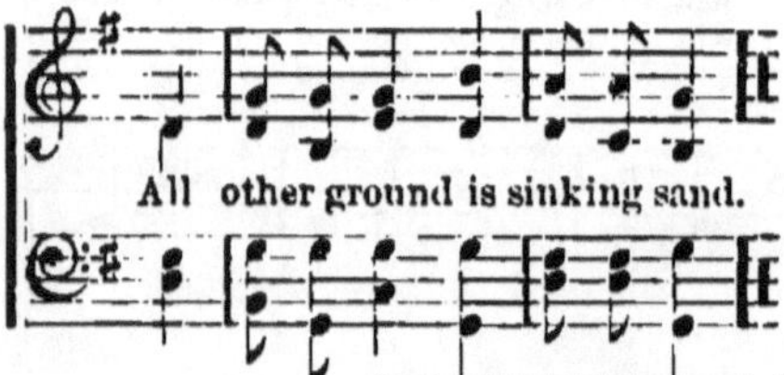

1. My hope is built on nothing less Than Jesus' blood and righteousness;
I dare not trust the sweetest frame, But wholly lean on Jesus' name:

On Christ, the Sol-id Rock, I stand; All oth-er ground is sinking sand,
All other ground is sinking sand.

2. When darkness seems to veil his face,
I rest on his unchanging grace;
In every high and stormy gale,
My anchor holds within the vale.

3. His oath, his covenant, and blood,
Support me in the whelming flood:
When all around my soul gives way,
He then is all my hope and stay.

Copyright, 1864, in "Golden Censer." Used by permission of Biglow & Main.

210. Oh, Sing to me of Heaven.

1. Oh, sing to me of heaven, When I'm a-bout to die,
2. When cold and slug-gish drops Roll off my mar-ble brow,

Cho.—There'll be no sor-row there, There'll be no sor-row there,

D. C.

Sing songs of ho-ly ec-sta-cy, To waft my soul on high!
Break forth in songs of joy-ful-ness, Let heaven be-gin be-low.

In heaven a-bove, where all is love, There'll be no sor-row there.

3 When the last moment comes,
    Oh, watch my dying face,
To catch the bright, seraphic gleam
    Which o'er my features plays.

4 Then to my raptured soul
    Let one sweet song be given,
Let music cheer me last on earth,
    And greet me first in heaven.

5 Then close my sightless eyes,
    And lay me down to rest,
And fold my pale and icy hands
    Upon my lifeless breast.

6 Then, round my senseless clay
    Assemble those I love,
And sing of heaven, delightful heaven,
    My glorious home above.

211. Abide with Me.

H. F. Lyte.   Tune, EVENTIDE. 10s.

1. Abide with me! fast falls the eventide, The darkness deepens—Lord, with me abide! When other helpers fail, and comforts flee, Help of the helpless, O abide with me!

2 Swift to its close ebbs out life's little day;
Earth's joys grow dim, its glories pass away;
Change and decay in all around I see;
O thou, who changest not, abide with me!

3 I need thy presence every passing hour;
What but thy grace can foil the tempter's power?
Who, like thyself, my guide and stay can be?
Through cloud and sunshine, Lord, abide with me!

4 I fear no foe, with thee at hand to bless;
Ills have no weight, and tears no bitterness;
Where is death's sting? where, grave, thy victory?
I triumph still, if thou abide with me.

5 Hold thou thy cross before my closing eyes;
Shine through the gloom and point me to the skies,
Heaven's morning breaks, and earth's vain shadows flee;
In life, in death, O Lord, abide with me!

Chant, ASPINWALL.

1. Abide with me! fast falls the eventide, The darkness deepens—Lord, with me abide! When other helpers fail, and comforts flee, Help of the helpless, O abide with me!

2 Where the saints, robed in white,
  Cleansed in life's flowing fountain,
  Shining beauteous and bright,
  They inhabit the mountain;
  Where no sin nor dismay,
  Neither trouble nor sorrow,
  Will be felt for a day,
  Nor be feared for the morrow.

3 He's prepared thee a home,—
  Sinner, canst thou believe it?
  And invites thee to come,—
  Sinner, wilt thou receive it?
  Oh, come, sinner, come,
  For the tide is receding;
  And the Saviour will soon
  And forever cease pleading.

218. He is Calling.

Faber.   Arr by S. J. Vail.

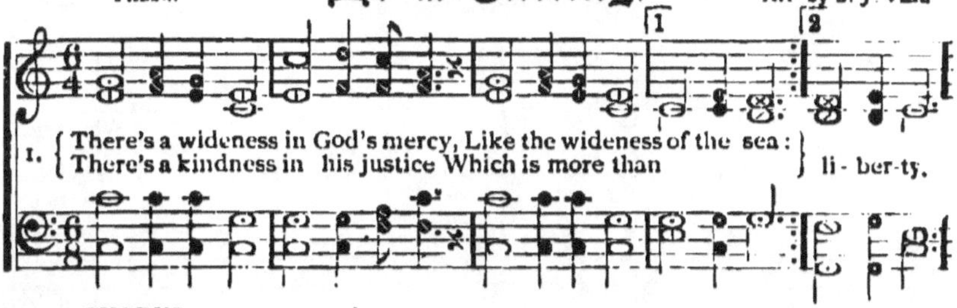

1. There's a wideness in God's mercy, Like the wideness of the sea:
There's a kindness in his justice Which is more than li-ber-ty.

CHORUS.
He is call-ing, "Come to me!" Lord, I'll gladly haste to thee.

2. There is welcome for the sinner,
And more graces for the good;
There is mercy with the Saviour;
There is healing in his blood.

3. For the love of God is broader
Than the measure of man's mind;

And the heart of the Eternal
Is most wonderful and kind.

4. If our love were but more simple,
We should take him at his word;
And our lives would be all sunshine
In the sweetness of our Lord.

219. The Golden Key.

"Prayer is the key to unlock the door, and the bolt to shut in the night."   J. R. S.

1. Prayer is the key For the bending knee To open the morn's first hours;
2. Not a soul so sad, Nor a heart so glad, When cometh the shades of night,
3. Take the golden key In your hand and see, As the night tide drifts away,

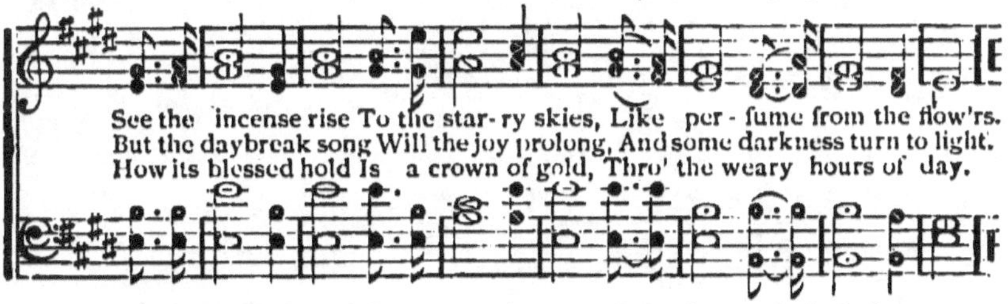

See the incense rise To the star-ry skies, Like per-fume from the flow'rs.
But the daybreak song Will the joy prolong, And some darkness turn to light.
How its blessed hold Is a crown of gold, Thro' the weary hours of day.

4. When the shadows fall,
And the vesper call
Is sobbing its low refrain,
'Tis a garland sweet
To the toil dent feet,
And an antidote for pain.

5. Soon the year's dark door
Shall be shut no more:
Life's tears shall be wiped away
As the pearl gates swing,
And the gold harps ring,
And the sun unsheathe for aye.

From "Goodly Pearls," by per.   211

220. Heaven is Propitious.

Arranged by ED.

1. Drooping souls, no longer grieve, Heaven is pro-pi-tious;
   If on Christ you do be-lieve, You will find him precious.
   D.C. He has died for you and I, Now look up and view him.

   Je-sus now is pass-ing by, Call-ing sin-ners to him;

2 From his hands, his feet, his side,
   Flows a healing fountain;
   See the consolation tide,
   Boundless as the ocean.
   See the living waters move,
   For the sick and dying;
   Now resolve to gain his love,
   Or to perish trying.

3 Streaming mercy, how it flows,
   Now I know, I feel it;
   Half has never yet been told,
   Yet I want to tell it.
   Jesus' blood has healed my wounds,
   Oh, the wondrous story!
   I was lost, but now am found,
   Glory! glory! glory!

221. Depth of Mercy.

J. STEVENSON.

1. Depth of mer-cy! can there be Mer-cy still re-served for me?
   Can my God his wrath for-bear, Me, the chief of sinners, spare?

CHORUS. Smoothly. Repeat pp.

God is love, I do believe;
He is waiting to forgive, He is wait-ing, waiting to for-give.

2 I have long withstood his grace;
  Long provoked him to his face;
  Would not hearken to his calls;
  Grieved him by a thousand falls.

3 Now incline me to repent;
  Let me now my sins lament;
  Now my soul revolt deplore,
  Weep, believe, and sin no more.

4 Kindled his relentings are;
  Me he now delights to spare;
  Cries, "How shall I give thee up?"
  Lets the lifted thunder drop.

5 There for me the Saviour stands,
  Shows his wounds and spreads his hands;
  God is love! I know, I feel;
  Jesus weeps, and loves me still.

222. Cleansing Wave.

Mrs. J. F. Knapp.

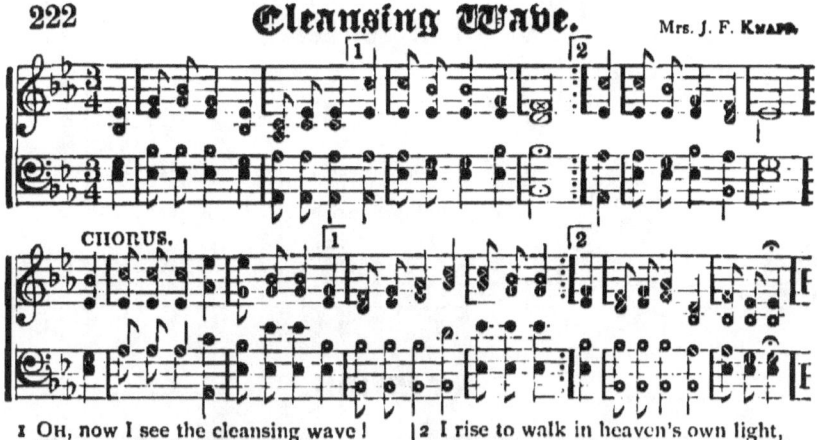

1 Oh, now I see the cleansing wave!
  The fountain deep and wide;
  Jesus, my Lord, mighty to save,
  Points to his wounded side.
Cho.—The cleansing stream, I see, I see!
  I plunge, and oh, it cleanseth me!
  Oh, praise the Lord! it cleanseth me;
  It cleanseth me—yes, cleanseth me.

2 I rise to walk in heaven's own light,
  Above the world of sin,
  With heart made pure and garments white,
  And Christ enthroned within.

3 Amazing grace! 'tis heaven below
  To feel the blood applied;
  And Jesus, only Jesus, know,
  My Jesus crucified.

223. Doxology.

Words arr. by B. M. A.   Melody by J. R. S.   Harmony by W. J. K.

Slow, with dignity.

Glo - ry be to the Fa - ther, Glo - ry be to the Son,

Glo - ry be to the Ho - ly Ghost; As it was in the be - ginning,

Is now, and ev - er shall be, World without end. A - men, a - men.

O Holy Saviour!—CONCLUDED.

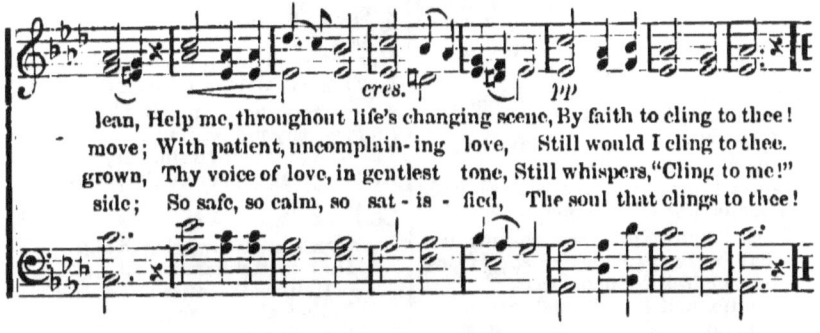

lean, Help me, throughout life's changing scene, By faith to cling to thee!
move; With patient, uncomplain-ing love, Still would I cling to thee.
grown, Thy voice of love, in gentlest tone, Still whispers, "Cling to me!"
side; So safe, so calm, so sat-is-fied, The soul that clings to thee!

227. Beyond the Smiling.

H. BONAR.   W. A. TARBUTTON.

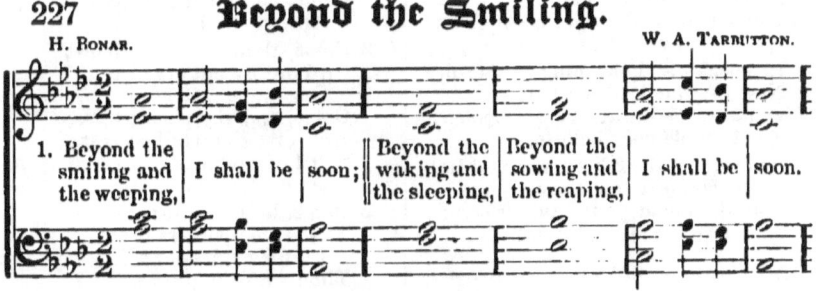

1. Beyond the smiling and the weeping, I shall be soon; Beyond the waking and the sleeping, Beyond the sowing and the reaping, I shall be soon.

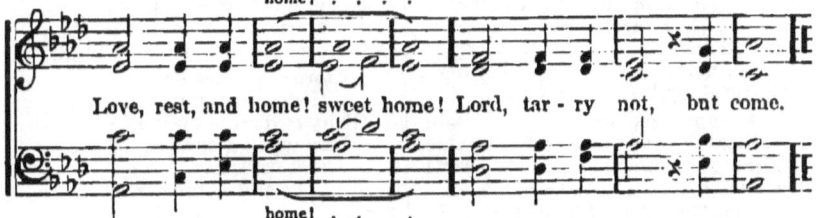

Love, rest, and home! sweet home! Lord, tar-ry not, but come.
home! . . .

1 Beyond the smiling and the weeping, |
    I shall be soon; ||
Beyond the waking and the sleeping, |
Beyond the sowing and the reaping, |
    I shall be soon. ||

2 Beyond the blooming and the fading, |
    I shall be soon; ||
Beyond the shining and the shading, |
Beyond the hoping and the dreading, |
    I shall be soon. ||

3 Beyond the rising and the setting, |
    I shall be soon; ||
Beyond the calming and the fretting, |
Beyond remembering and forgetting, |
    I shall be soon. ||

4 Beyond the parting and the meeting, |
    I shall be soon; ||
Beyond the farewell and the greeting, |
Beyond the pulse's fever beating, |
    I shall be soon. ||

5 Beyond the frost-chain and the fever, |
    I shall be soon; ||
Beyond the rock-waste and the river, |
Beyond the ever and the never, |
    I shall be soon. ||

228 C. M. M. B. H. I.

O FOR a thousand tongues, to sing
  My great Redeemer's praise;
The glories of my God and King,
  The triumphs of his grace!

2 My gracious Master and my God,
  Assist me to proclaim,
To spread through all the earth abroad,
  The honors of thy name.

3 Jesus! the name that charms our
  That bids our sorrows cease; [fears,
'Tis music in the sinners ears,
  'Tis life, and health, and peace.

4 He breaks the power of canceled sin,
  He sets the prisoner free;
His blood can make the foulest clean;
  His blood availed for me.

5 He speaks, and, listening to his voice,
  New life the dead receive;
The mournful broken hearts rejoice;
  The humble poor believe.

6 Hear him, ye deaf; his praise, ye dumb,
  Your loosened tongues employ;
Ye blind, behold your Saviour come;
  And leap, ye lame, for joy.

229 C.P.M. M. B. H. 18.

THOU God of power, thou God of love,
Whose glory fills the realms above,
  Whose praise archangels sing,
And veil their faces while they cry,
"Thrice holy," to their God most high,
  "Thrice holy," to their King;

2 Thee as our God we too would claim,
And bless the Saviour's precious name,
  Through whom this grace is given;
He bore the curse to sinners due,
He forms their ruined souls anew,
  And makes them heirs of heaven.

3 The veil that hides thy glory rend,
And here in saving power descend,
  And fix thy blest abode;
Here to our hearts thyself reveal,
And let each waiting spirit feel
  The presence of our God.

230 L. M. M. B. H. 12.

JESUS, thou everlasting King,
Accept the tribute which we bring;
Accept thy well-deserved renown,
And wear our praises as thy crown.

2 Let every act of worship be
Like our espousals, Lord, to thee;
Like the blest hour when from above
We first received the pledge of love.

3 The gladness of that happy day,
O may it over, ever stay!
Nor let our faith forsake its hold,
Nor hope decline, nor love grow cold.

4 Let every moment as it flies,
Increase thy praise, improve our joys,
Till we are raised to sing thy name
At the great supper of the Lamb.

231 6, 4. M. B. H. 6

COME, thou almighty King,
Help us thy name to sing,
  Help us to praise:
Father all-glorious,
O'er all victorious,
Come, and reign over us,
  Ancient of days!

2 Come, thou incarnate Word,
Gird on thy mighty sword,
  Our prayer attend;
Come, and thy people bless,
And give thy word success:
Spirit of holiness,
  On us descend!

3 Come, holy Comforter,
Thy sacred witness bear
  In this glad hour:
Thou who almighty art,
Now rule in every heart,
And ne'er from us depart,
  Spirit of power!

4 To thee, great One and Three,
Eternal praises be
  Hence, evermore:
Thy sovereign majesty
May we in glory see,
And to eternity
  Love and adore!

232 C. M. M. R. H. 2.

COME, let us join our cheerful songs
  With angels round the throne;
Ten thousand thousand are their
  But all their joys are one. [tongues,

2 "Worthy the Lamb that died," they
  "To be exalted thus!" [cry.
"Worthy the Lamb!" our hearts reply,
  "For he was slain for us."

3 Jesus is worthy to receive
  Honor and power divine;
And blessings more than we can give,
  Be, Lord, forever thine.

4 The whole creation join in one,
  To bless the sacred name
Of him that sits upon the throne,
  And to adore the Lamb.

233 L. M. M. R. H. 44.
JESUS, where'er thy people meet,
 There they behold thy mercy-seat;
Where'er they seek thee thou art
  found,
And every place is hallowed ground.
2 For thou, within no walls confined,
 Dost dwell with those of humble mind;
Such ever bring thee where they come,
And, going, take thee to their home.
3 Great Shepherd of thy chosen few,
 Thy former mercies here renew;
Here, to our waiting hearts proclaim
The sweetness of thy saving name.
4 Here may we prove the power of
  prayer
To strengthen faith and sweeten care;
To teach our faint desires to rise,
And bring all heaven before our eyes.

234 7s. M. R. H. 21.
LORD, we come before thee now,
 At thy feet we humbly bow;
O do not our suit disdain,
Shall we seek thee, Lord, in vain?
2 Lord, on thee our souls depend;
 In compassion now descend;
Fill our hearts with thy rich grace,
Tune our lips to sing thy praise.
3 In thine own appointed way
 Now we seek thee, here we stay;
Lord, we know not how to go
Till a blessing thou bestow.
4 Send some message from thy word
 That may joy and peace afford;
Let thy Spirit now impart
Full salvation to each heart.
5 Comfort those who weep and mourn,
 Let the time of joy return;
Those that are cast down lift up,
Make them strong in faith and hope.
6 Grant that all may seek and find
 Thee a gracious God and kind:
Heal the sick, the captive free;
Let us all rejoice in thee.

235 C. M. M. R. H. 32.
JESUS, thou all redeeming Lord,
 Thy blessing we implore;
Open the door to preach thy word,
 The great effectual door.
2 Gather the outcasts in, and save
 From sin and Satan's power;
And let them now acceptance have,
 And know their gracious hour.

3 Lover of souls! thou know'st to prize
 What thou hast bought so dear:
Come, then, and in thy people's eyes
 With all thy wounds appear.
4 The hardness of our hearts remove,
 Thou who for all hast died;
Show us the tokens of thy love,
 Thy feet, thy hands, thy side.
5 Ready thou art the blood to apply,
 And prove the record true;
And all thy wounds to sinners cry,
 "I suffered this for you."

236 8, 7, 4. M. R. H. 54.
IN thy name, O Lord, assembling,
 We, thy people, now draw near;
Teach us to rejoice with trembling;
 Speak and let thy servants hear:
   Hear with meekness,
 Hear thy word with godly fear.
2 While our days on earth are length-
   ened,
 May we give them, Lord, to thee:
Cheered by hope, and daily strength-
May we run, nor weary be, [ened,
   Till thy glory
 Without cloud in heaven we see.
3 There, in worship purer, sweeter,
 All thy people shall adore;
Sharing then in rapture greater
 Than they could conceive before:
   Full enjoyment,
 Full and pure, forevermore.

237 C. M. M. R. H. 60.
LORD, when we bend before thy throne,
 And our confessions pour,
O may we feel the sins we own,
 And hate what we deplore.
2 Our contrite spirits pitying see;
 True penitence impart;
And let a healing ray from thee
 Beam peace into each heart.
3 When we disclose our wants in prayer,
 May we our wills resign;
And not a thought our bosom share
 Which is not wholly thine.
4 And when, with heart and voice, we
 Our grateful hymns to raise, [strive,
Let love divine within us live,
 And fill our souls with praise.
5 Then, on thy glories while we dwell,
 Thy mercies we'll review;
With love divine transported, tell —
 Thou, God, art Father too!

238 C. M. M. R. H. 63.

Come, ye that love the Saviour's name,
 And joy to make it known,
The Sovereign of your hearts proclaim,
 And bow before his throne.

2 Behold your Lord, your Master,
 With glories all divine;' [crowned
And tell the wondering nations round
 How bright those glories shine.

3 When, in his earthly courts, we view
 The glories of our King,
We long to love as angels do,
 And wish like them to sing.

4 And shall we long and wish in vain?
 Lord, teach our songs to rise :
Thy love can animate the strain,
 And bid it reach the skies.

239 L. M. M. R H. 39.

Thy presence, gracious God, afford ;
Prepare us to receive thy word :
Now let thy voice engage our ear,
And faith be mixed with what we hear.

2 Distracting thoughts and cares remove,
And fix our hearts and hopes above ;
With food divine may we be fed,
And satisfied with l ving bread.

3 To us the sacred word a ply
With sovereign power and energy ;
And may we, in thy faith and fear,
Reduce to practice what we hear.

4 Father, in us thy Son reveal ;
Teach us to know and do thy will ;
Thy saving power and love display,
And guide us to the realms of day.

240 S. M. M. E. H. 41.

Come, ye that love the Lord,
 And let your j ys be known :
Join in a song with sweet accord,
 While ye surround his throne.

2 Let those refuse to sing
 Who never knew our God,
But servants of the heavenly King
 May speak their joys abroad.

3 The God that rules on high,
 That all the earth surveys,
That rides upon the stormy sky,
 And calms the roaring seas ;

4 This awful God is ours,
 Our Father and our Love ;
He will send down his heavenly
 To carry us above. [powers,

5 There we shall see his face,
 And never, never sin ;
There, from the rivers of his grace,
 Drink endless pleasures in :

6 Yea, and before we rise
 To that immortal state,
The thoughts of such amazing bliss
 Should constant joys create.

7 The men of grace have found
 Glory begun below ;
Celestial fruit on earthly ground
 From faith and hope may grow :

8 Then let our songs abound,
 And every tear be dry ; [ground,
We're marching through Immanuel's
 To fairer worlds on high.

241 L. M. M. R. H. 8.

From all that dwell below the skies,
Let the Creator's praise arise ;
Let the Redeemer's name be sung,
Through every land, by every tongue.

2 Eternal are thy mercies, Lord ;
Eternal truth attends thy word :
Thy praise shall sound from shore to shore,
Till suns shall rise and set no more.

3 Your lofty themes, ye mortals, bring ;
In songs of praise divinely sing ;
The great salvation loud proclaim,
And shout for joy the Saviour's name.

4 In every land begin the song :
To every land the strains belong :
In cheerful sounds all voices raise,
And fill the world with loudest praise.

242 L. M. M. R. H. 81.

Sweet is the work, my God, my King,
To praise thy name, give thanks, and sing ;
To show thy love by morning l'ght,
And talk of all thy truth by night.

2 Sweet is the day of sacred rest ;
No mortal cares shall seize my breast ;
O may my heart in tune be found,
Like David's harp of solemn sound.

3 When grace has purified my heart,
Then I shall share a glorious part ;
And fresh supplies of joy be shed,
Like holy oil, to cheer my head.

4 Then shall I see, and hear, and know
All I desired or wished below ;
And every power find sweet employ
In that eternal world of joy.

243 L. M. M. E. H. 66.

Come, let us tune our loftiest song,
  And raise to Christ our joyful strain:
Worship and thanks to him belong,
  Who reigns and shall forever reign.

2 His sovereign power our bodies made;
  Our souls are his immortal breath:
And when his creatures sinned he bled,
  To save us from eternal death.

3 Burn, every breast, with Jesus' love;
  Bound, every heart, with rapturous joy;
And, saints on earth, with saints above
  Your voices in his praise employ.

4 Extol the Lamb with loftiest song,
  Ascend for him, our cheerful strain;
Worship and thanks to him belong,
  Who reigns and shall forever reign.

244 L. M. M. E. H. 102.

Sun of my soul thou Saviour dear,
It is not night if thou be near:
O may no earthborn cloud arise
To hide thee from thy servant's eyes.

2 When the soft dews of kindly sleep
My wearied eyelids gently steep,
Be my last thought, how sweet to rest
Forever on my Saviour's breast.

3 Abide with me from morn till eve,
For without thee I cannot live;
Abide with me when night is nigh,
For without thee I dare not die.

4 If some poor wandering child of thine
Have spurned, to-day, the voice divine,
Now, Lord, the gracious work begin ;
Let him no more lie down in sin.

5 Watch by the sick; enrich the poor
With blessings from thy boundless store;
Be every mourner's sleep to-night,
Like infant's slumbers, pure and light.

6 Come near and bless us when we wake,
Ere through the world our way we take;
Till in the ocean of thy love
We lose ourselves in heaven above.

245 S. M. M. E. H. 176.

How gentle God's commands!
  How kind his precepts are!
Come, cast your burdens on the Lord,
  And trust his constant care.

2 Beneath his watchful eye
  His saints securely dwell;
That hand which bears all nature up
  Shall guard his children well.

3 Why should this anxious load
  Press down your weary mind?
Haste to your heavenly Father's throne,
  And sweet refreshment find.

4 His goodness stands approved,
  Unchanged from day to day:
I'll drop my burden at his feet,
  And bear a song away.

246 11, 12, 10. M. E. H. 136.

Holy, holy, holy, Lord God Almighty!
Early in the morning our song shall rise to thee;
Holy, holy, holy, merciful and mighty,
God in Three Persons, blessed Trinity!

2 Holy, holy, holy! all the saints adore thee,
Casting down their golden crowns around the glassy sea;
Cherubim and seraphim falling down before thee, [be.
Which wert and art and evermore shalt

3 Holy, holy, holy! though the darkness hide thee,
Though the eye of sinful man thy glory may not see; [thee,
Only thou art holy; there is none beside
Perfect in power, in love and purity.

4 Holy, holy, holy, Lord God Almighty!
All thy works shall praise thy name,
  in earth, and sky, and sea;
Holy, holy, holy, merciful and mighty,
God in Three Persons, blessed Trinity!

247 L. M. M. E. H. 69.

Great God, attend, while Zion sings
The joy that from thy presence springs;
To spend one day with thee on earth
Exceeds a thousand days of mirth.

2 Might I enjoy the meanest place
Within thy house, O God of grace,
Not tent of ease, nor thrones of power,
Should tempt my feet to leave thy door.

3 God is our sun, he makes our day;
God is our shield, he guards our way
From all assaults of hell and sin,
From foes without, and foes within.

4 All needful grace will God bestow,
And crown that grace with glory too;
He gives us all things, and withholds
No real good from upright souls.

5 O God, our King, whose sovereign sway
The glorious hosts of heaven obey,
And devils at thy presence flee;
Blest is the man that trusts in thee.

248   C. M.   M. E. H. 183.
Joy to the world! the Lord is come;
  Let earth receive her King;
Let every heart prepare him room,
  And heaven and nature sing.

2 Joy to the world! the Saviour reigns;
  Let men their songs employ;
While fields and floods, rocks, hills, and
  Repeat the sounding joy. [plains,

3 No more let sin and sorrow grow,
  Nor thorns infest the ground;
He comes to make his blessings flow
  Far as the curse is found.

4 He rules the world with truth and
  And makes nations prove [grace,
The glories of his righteousness,
  And wonders of his love.

249   C. M.   M. E. H. 125.
O God, thy power is wonderful,
  Thy glory passing bright;
Thy wisdom, with its deep on deep,
  A rapture to the sight.

2 I see thee in the eternal years
  In glory all alone,
Ere round thine uncreated fires
  Created light had shone.

3 I see thee walk in Eden's shade,
  I see thee all through time;
Thy patience and compassion seem
  New attributes sublime.

4 I see thee when the doom is o'er,
  And outworn time is done,
Still, still incomprehensible,
  O God, yet not alone.

5 Angelic spirits, countless souls,
  Of thee have drunk their fill;
And to eternity will drink
  Thy joy and glory still.

6 O little heart of mine! shall pain
  Or sorrow make thee moan,
When all this God is all for thee,
  A Father all thine own?

250   L. M.   M. E. H. 168.
God is our refuge and defense;
  In trouble our unfailing aid:
Secure in his omnipotence,
  What foe can make our souls afraid?

2 Yea, tho' the earth's foundations rock,
  And mountains down the gulf be hurled,
His people smile amid the shock:
  They look beyond this transient world.

3 There is a river pure and bright,
  Whose streams make glad the heaven-
Where, in eternity of light; [ly plains;
  The city of our God remains.

4 Built by the word of his command,
  With his unclouded presence blest,
Firm as his throne the bulwarks stand;
  There is our home, our hope, our rest.

251   8, 7, 4.   M. E. H. 171.
Guide me, O thou great Jehovah,
  Pilgrim through this barren land:
I am weak, but thou art mighty;
  Hold me with thy powerful hand:
    Bread of heaven,
Feed me till I want no more.

2 Open now the crystal fountain,
  Whence the healing waters flow;
Let the fiery, cloudy pillar,
  Lead me all my journey through:
    Strong Deliverer,
Be thou still my strength and shield.

3 When I tread the verge of Jordan,
  Bid my anxious fears subside;
Bear me through the swelling current;
  Land me safe on Canaan's side:
    Songs of praises
I will ever give to thee.

252   C. M.   M. E. H. 161.
God moves in a mysterious way
  His wonders to perform;
He plants his footsteps in the sea,
  And rides upon the storm.

2 Deep in unfathomable mines
  Of never-failing skill,
He treasures up his bright designs,
  And works his sovereign will.

3 Ye fearful saints, fresh courage take;
  The clouds ye so much dread
Are big with mercy, and shall break
  In blessings on your head.

4 Judge not the Lord by feeble sense,
  But trust him for his grace;
Behind a frowning providence
  He hides a smiling face.

5 His purposes will ripen fast,
  Unfolding every hour:
The bud may have a bitter taste,
  But sweet will be the flower.

6 Blind unbelief is sure to err,
  And scan his work in vain:
God is his own interpreter,
  And he will make it plain.

253. C. M. M. E. H. 147.

1 My God, how wonderful thou art,
   Thy majesty how bright,
   How beautiful thy mercy-seat
   In depths of burning light!

2 How dread are thine eternal years,
   O everlasting Lord,
   By prostrate spirits day and night
   Incessantly adored!

3 How beautiful, now beautiful,
   The sight of thee must be,
   Thine endless wisdom, boundless
      power,
   And awful purity!

4 O how I fear thee, living God,
   With deepest, tenderest fears,
   And worship thee with trembling hope,
   And penitential tears.

5 Yet I may love thee too, O Lord,
   Almighty as thou art:
   For thou hast stooped to ask of me
   The love of my poor heart.

6 No earthly father loves like thee,
   No mother half so mild
   Bears and forbears as thou hast done
   With me, thy sinful child.

7 Father of Jesus, love's reward!
   What rapture will it be,
   Prostrate before thy throne to lie,
   And gaze, and gaze on thee!

254. L. M. M. R. H. 164.

1 Peace, troubled soul, thou need'st not
      fear;
   Thy great Provider still is near;
   Who fed thee la t, will feed thee still:
   Be calm, and sink into his will.

2 The Lord, who built the earth and sky,
   In mercy stoops to hear thy cry;
   His promise all may freely claim;
   Ask and reeive in Jesus' name.

3 Without reserve give Christ your
      heart;
   Let him his righteousness impart;
   Then all things else he'll freely give;
   With him you all things shall receive.

4 Thus shall the soul be truly blest,
   That seeks in God his only rest;
   May I that happy person be,
   In time and in eternity.

255. L. M. M. R. H. 170.

1 How do thy mercies close me round!
   Forever be thy name adored;
   I blush in all things to abound;
   The servant is above his Lord.

2 Inured to poverty and pain,
   A suffering life my Master led;
   The Son of God the Son of man,
   He had not where to lay his head.

3 But lo! a place he hath prepared
   For me, whom watchful angels keep;
   Yea, he himself becomes my guard;
   He smooths my bed, and gives me sleep.

4 Jesus protects; my fears, be gone:
   What can the Rock of ages move?
   Safe in thy arms I lay me down,
   Thine everlasting arms of love.

5 While thou art int'mately nigh,
   Who, who shall violate my rest?
   Sin, earth, and hell I now defy:
   I lean upon my Saviour's breast.

6 I rest beneath the Almighty's shade;
   My griefs expire, my troubles cease;
   Thou, Lord, on whom my soul is stayed,
   Wilt keep me still in perfect peace.

256. C. M. M. R. H. 185.

1 Hark, the glad sound! the Saviour
      comes,
   The Saviour promised long;
   Let every heart prepare a throne,
   And every voice a song.

2 He comes, the prisoner to release,
   In Satan's bondage held;
   The gates of brass before him burst,
   The iron fetters yield.

3 He comes from thickest films of vice
   To clear the mental ray,
   And on the eyes oppressed with night
   To pour celestial day.

4 He comes, the broken heart to bind,
   The wounded soul to cure,
   And with the treasures of his grace,
   To enrich the humble poor.

5 Our glad hosannas, Prince of Peace,
   Thy welcome shall proclaim,
   And heaven's eternal arches ring
   With thy beloved name.

257. 8s. M. E. H. 143.

1 This God is the God we adore,
   Our faithful, unchangeable friend,
   Whose love is as great as his power,
   And neither knows measure nor end:

2 'Tis Jesus, the first and the last,
   Whose spirit shall guide us safe home;
   We'll praise him for all that is past,
   And trust him for all that's to come.

258   L. M.   M. E. H. 239.

Jesus, my Advocate above,
My Friend before the throne of love,
If now for me prevails thy prayer,
If now I find thee pleading there,—

2 If thou the secret wish convey,
And sweetly prompt my heart to pray,—
Hear, and my weak petitions join,
Almighty Advocate, to thine.

3 Jesus, my heart's desire obtain;
My earnest suit present, and gain:
My fulness of corruption show;
The knowledge of myself bestow.

4 O sovereign Love, to thee I cry,
Give me thyself, or else I die!
Save me from death, from hell set free;
Death, hell, are but the want of thee.

259   L. M.   M. E. H. 242.

I KNOW that my Redeemer lives;
What joy the blest assurance gives!
He lives, he lives, who once was dead;
He lives, my everlasting Head!

2 He lives to bless me with his love;
He lives, to plead for me above;
He lives, my hungry soul to feed;
He lives, to help in time of need.

3 He lives, and grants me daily breath;
He lives, and I shall conquer death;
He lives, my mansion to prepare;
He lives, to bring me safely there.

4 He lives, all glory to his name;
He lives, my Saviour, still the same;
What joy the blest assurance gives,
I know that my Redeemer lives!

260   8,7. d.   M. E. H. 246.

HAIL, thou once despised Jesus!
Hail, thou Galilean King!
Thou didst suffer to release us;
Thou didst free salvation bring.
Hail, thou agonizing Saviour,
Bearer of our sin and shame!
By thy merits we find favor;
Life is given through thy name.

2 Paschal Lamb, by God appointed,
All our sins on thee were laid:
By almighty love annointed,
Thou hast full atonement made.
All thy people are forgiven,
Through the virtue of thy blood;
Opened is the gate of heaven;
Peace is made 'twixt man and God.

3 Jesus, hail! enthroned in glory,
There forever to abide;
All the heavenly hosts adore thee,
Seated at thy Father's side;
There for sinners thou art pleading;
There thou dost our place prepare
Ever for us interceding,
Till in glory we appear.

4 Worship, honor, power, and blessing,
Thou art worthy to receive;
Loudest praises, without ceasing,
Meet it is for us to give.
Help, ye bright angelic spirits;
Bring your sweetest, noblest lays;
Help to sing our Saviour's merits;
Help to chant Immanuel's praise!

261   L. M.   M. E. H. 213.

WHEN I survey the wondrous cross
On which the Prince of glory died,
My richest gain I count but loss,
And pour contempt on all my pride.

2 Forbid it, Lord, that I should boast,
Save in the death of Christ, my God;
All the vain things that charm me most,
I sacrifice them to his blood.

3 See, from his head, his hands, his feet,
Sorrow and love flow mingled down:
Did e'er such love and sorrow meet,
Or thorns compose so rich a crown?

4 Were the whole realm of nature mine,
That were a present far too small;
Love so amazing, so divine,
Demands my soul, my life, my all.

262   C. M.   M. E. H. 214.

ALAS! and did my Saviour bleed?
And did my sovereign die?
Would he devote that sacred head
For such a worm as I?

2 Was it for crimes that I have done,
He groaned upon the tree?
Amazing pity! grace unknown!
And love beyond degree!

3 Well might the sun in darkness hide,
And shut his glories in,
When Christ, the mighty Maker, died,
For man, the creature's sin.

4 Thus might I hide my blushing face
While his dear cross appears;
Dissolve my heart in thankfulness,
And melt mine eyes to tears.

5 But drops of grief can ne'er repay
The debt of love I owe:
Here, Lord, I give myself away,—
'Tis all that I can do.

263 8,7. M. E. H. 204.

In the cross of Christ I glory,
Towering o'er the wrecks of time;
All the light of sacred story
Gathers round its head sublime.

2 When the woes of life o'ertake me,
Hopes deceive, and fears annoy,
Never shall the cross forsake me;
Lo! it glows with peace and joy.

3 When the sun of bliss is beaming
Light and love upon my way,
From the cross the radiance streaming
Adds more luster to the day.

4 Bane and blessing, pain and pleasure,
By the cross are sanctified;
Peace is there that knows no measure,
Joys that through all time abide.

5 In the cross of Christ I glory,
Towering o'er the wrecks of time;
All the light of sacred story
Gathers round its head sublime.

264 7s. M. E. H. 205.

Never further than thy cross:
Never higher than thy feet:
Here earth's precious things seem dross:
Here earth's bitter things grow sweet.

2 Gazing thus our sin we see,
Learn thy love while gazing thus;
Sin, which laid the cross on thee,
Love, which bore the cross for us.

3 Here we learn to serve and give,
And, rejoicing, self deny;
Here we gather love to live,
Here we gather faith to die.

4 Pressing onward as we can,
Still to this our hearts must tend;
Where our earliest hopes began,
There our last aspirings end;

5 Till amid the hosts of light,
We in thee redeemed, complete,
Through thy cross made pure and white,
Cast our crowns before thy feet.

265 L. M. M. E. H. 234.

He dies! the Friend of sinners dies!
Lo! Salem's daughters weep around;
A solemn darkness veils the skies,
A sudden trembling shakes the ground.

2 Come, saints, and drop a tear or two
For him who groaned beneath your load;
He shed a thousand drops for you,—
A thousand drops of richer blood.

3 Here's love and grief beyond degree,
The Lord of glory dies for man!
But lo! what sudden joys we see,
Jesus, the dead, revives again!

4 The rising God forsakes the tomb;
In vain the tomb forbids his rise,
Cherubic legions guard him home,
And shout him welcome to the skies.

5 Break off your tears, ye saints, and tell
How high your great Deliverer reigns;
Sing how he spoiled the hosts of hell,
And lead the monster Death in chains·

6 Say, "Live forever, wondrous King!
Born to redeem, and strong to save;"
Then ask the monster, "Where's thy sting?"
And, "Where's thy victory, boasting Grave?"

266 7s. M. E. H. 262.

Gracious Spirit, Love divine,
Let thy light within me shine!
All my guilty fears remove;
Fill me with thy heavenly love.

2 Speak thy pardoning grace to me;
Set the burdened sinner free;
Lead me to the Lamb of God;
Wash me in his precious blood.

3 Life and peace to me impart;
Seal salvation on my heart;
Breathe thyself into my breast,
Earnest of immortal rest.

5 Let me never from thee stray;
Keep me in the narrow way;
Fill my soul with joy divine;
Keep me, Lord, forever thine.

267 L. M. M. E. H. 307.

Jesus, a word, a look from thee,
Can turn my heart and make it clean;
Purge out the inbred leprosy,
And save me from my bosom sin.

2 Lord, if thou wilt, I do believe,
Thou canst the saving grace impart;
Thou canst this instant now forgive,
And stamp thine image on my heart.

3 My heart, which now to thee I raise,
I know thou canst this moment cleanse;
The deepest stains of sin efface,
And drive the evil spirit hence.

4 Be it according to thy word;
Accomplish now thy work in me:
And let my soul, to health restored,
Devote its deathless powers to thee.

268   S. M.   M. E. H. 312.

Our sins on Christ were laid;
  He bore the mighty load;
Our ransom-price he fully paid
  In groans, and tears, and blood.

2 To save a world, he dies;
  Sinners, behold the Lamb!
To him lift up your longing eyes;
  Seek mercy in his name.

3 Pardon and peace abound;
  He will your sins forgive;
Salvation in his name is found—
  He bids the sinner live.

4 Jesus, we look to thee;
  Where else can sinners go?
Thy boundless love shall set us free
  From wretchedness and woe.

269   11s.   M. E. H. 335.

O turn ye, O turn ye, for why will ye die,
When God in great mercy is coming so nigh?
Now Jesus invites you, the Spirit says, "Come,"
And angels are waiting to welcome you home.

2 And now Christ is ready your souls to receive,
O how can you question, if you will believe?
If sin is your burden, why will you not come?
'Tis you he bids welcome; he bids you come home.

3 In riches, in pleasures, what can you obtain,
To soothe your affliction, or banish your pain?
To bear up your spirit when summoned to die,
Or waft you to mansions of glory on high?

4 Why will you be starving, and feeding on air?
There's mercy in Jesus, enough and to spare;
If still you are doubting, make trial and see,
And prove that his mercy is boundless and free.

270   L. M.   M. E. H. 238.

Jesus, thy blood and righteousness
My beauty are, my glorious dress;
'Midst flaming worlds, in these arrayed,
With joy shall I lift up my head.

2 Bold shall I stand in thy great day,
For who aught to my charge shall lay?
Fully absolved through these I am,
From sin and fear, from guilt and shame.

3 The holy, meek, unspotted Lamb.
Who from the Father's bosom came,
Who died for me, e'en me to atone,
Now for my Lord and God I own.

4 Lord, I believe thy precious blood,
Which, at the mercy-seat of God,
Forever doth for sinners plead,
For me, e'en for my soul, was shed.

5 Lord, I believe were sinners more
Than sands upon the ocean shore,
Thou hast for all a ransom paid,
For all a full atonement made.

271   H. M.   M. E. H. 344

Rejoice, the Lord is King!
  Your Lord and King adore;
Mortals, give thanks and sing,
  And triumph evermore;
Lift up your hearts, lift up your voice,
Rejoice, again I say, rejoice.

2 Jesus, the Saviour, reigns,
  The God of truth and love;
When he had purged our stains,
  He took his seat above;
Lift up your hearts, lift up your voice;
Rejoice, again I say, rejoice.

3 His kingdom cannot fail,
  He rules o'er earth and heaven,
The keys of death and hell
  Are to our Jesus given;
Lift up your hearts, lift up your voice;
Rejoice, again I say, rejoice.

4 He sits at God's right hand
  Till all his foes submit,
And bow to his command,
  And fall beneath his feet;
Lift up your hearts, lift up your voice;
Rejoice, again I say, rejoice.

5 He all his foes shall quell,
  And all our sins destroy;
Let every bosom swell
  With pure, seraphic joy;
Lift up your hearts, lift up your voice;
Rejoice, again I say, rejoice.

6 Rejoice in glorious hope;
  Jesus, the Judge shall come,
And take his servants up
  To their eternal home;
We soon shall hear the archangel's voice!
The trump of God shall sound,—Rejoice;

272 C. M. M. E. H. 254.

With joy we meditate the grace
 Of our High Priest above;
His heart is made of tenderness,
 His bowels melt with love.

2 Touched with a sympathy within,
 He knows our feeble frame;
He knows what sore temptations mean,
 For he hath felt the same.

3 He, in the days of feeble flesh,
 Poured out strong cries and tears,
And in his measure feels afresh
 What every member bears.

4 He'll never quench the smoking flax,
 But raise it to a flame;
The bruised reed he never breaks,
 Nor scorns the meanest name.

5 Then let our humble faith address
 His mercy and his power;
We shall obtain delivering grace
 In every trying hour.

273 C. M. M. E. H. 277.

Come, Holy Spirit heavenly Dove,
 With all thy quickening powers;
Kindle a flame of sacred love
 In these cold hearts of ours.

2 Look how we grovel here below,
 Fond of these earthly toys;
Our souls, how heavily they go,
 To reach eternal joys.

3 In vain we tune our formal songs,
 In vain we strive to rise;
Hosannas languish on our tongues,
 And our devotion dies.

4 Father, and shall we ever live
 At this poor, dying rate,
Our love so faint, so cold to thee,
 And thine to us so great?

5 Come, Holy Spirit, heavenly Dove,
 With all thy quickening powers;
Come, shed abroad a Saviour's love,
 And that shall kindle ours.

274 C. M. M. E. H. 316.

How sweet the name of Jesus sounds
 In a believer's ear!
It soothes his sorrows, heals his wounds.
 And drives away his fear.

2 It makes the wounded spirit whole,
 And calms the troubled breast;
'Tis manna to the hungry soul,
 And to the weary, rest.

3 Dear name! the rock on which I build,
 My shield and hiding-place;
My never-failing treasure filled
 With boundless stores of grace!

4 Jesus, my Shepherd, Saviour, Friend,
 My Prophet, Priest, and King,
My Lord, my Life, my Way, my End,
 Accept the praise I bring!

5 I would thy boundless love proclaim
 With every fleeting breath;
So shall the music of thy name
 Refresh my soul in death.

275 C. M. M. E. H. 323.

O what amazing words of grace
 Are in the Gospel found!
Suited to every sinner's case,
 Who knows the joyful sound.

2 Poor, sinful, thirsty, fainting souls
 Are freely welcome here;
Salvation like a river rolls,
 Abundant, free, and clear.

3 Come, then, with all your wants and
 Your every burden bring: [wounds;
Here love, unchanging love, abounds,
 A deep, celestial spring.

4 Whoever will - O gracious word!
 May of this stream partake;
Come, thirsty souls, and bless the Lord,
 And drink, for Jesus' sake.

5 Millions of sinners, vile as you,
 Have here found life and peace;
Come, then, and prove its virtues too,
 And drink, adore, and bless.

276 7s. 6l. M. E. H. 415.

Rock of ages, cleft for me,
 Let me hide myself in thee;
Let the water and the blood,
 From thy wounded side which flowed,
Be of sin the double cure,
 Save from wrath and make me pure.

2 Could my tears forever flow,
 Could my zeal no languor know,
These for sin could not atone;
 Thou must save, and thou alone:
In my hand no price I bring;
 Simply to thy cross I cling.

3 While I draw this fleeting breath,
 When my eyes shall close in death,
When I rise to worlds unknown,
 And behold thee on thy throne,
Rock of ages, cleft for me,
 Let me hide myself in thee.

277 L. M. M. E. H. 305.

Lord, we are vile, conceived in sin,
And born unholy and unclean;
Sprung from the man whose guilty fall
Corrupts his race, and taints us all.

2 Soon as we draw our infant breath
The seeds of sin grow up for death:
Thy law demands a perfect heart,
But we're defiled in every part.

3 Behold, we fall before thy face;
Our only refuge is thy grace:
No outward forms can make us clean;
The leprosy lies deep within.

4 Nor bleeding bird, nor bleeding beast,
Nor hyssop branch, nor sprinkling priest,
Nor running brook, nor flood, nor sea,
Can wash the dismal stain away.

5 Jesus, thy blood, thy blood alone,
Hath power sufficient to atone;
Thy blood can make us white as snow,
No Jewish types could cleanse us so.

6 While guilt disturbs and breaks our peace,
Nor flesh nor soul hath rest or ease;
Lord, let us hear thy pardoning voice,
And make these broken hearts rejoice.

278 L. M. M. E. H. 327.

Of him who did salvation bring,
I could forever think and sing;
Arise, ye needy,—he'll relieve;
Arise, ye guilty,—he'll forgive.

2 Ask but his grace, and lo, 'tis given;
Ask, and he turns your hell to heaven:
Though sin and sorrow wound my soul,
Jesus, thy balm will make it whole.

3 To shame our sins he blushed in blood;
He closed his eyes to show us God:
Let all the world fall down and know
That none but God such love can show.

4 'Tis thee I love, for thee alone
I shed my tears and make my moan;
Where'er I am, where'er I move,
I meet the object of my love.

5 Insatiate to this spring I fly;
I drink, and yet am ever dry:
Ah! who against thy charms is proof?
Ah! who that loves can love enough?

279 7s. M. E. H. 345.

Hasten, sinner, to be wise!
  Stay not for the morrow's sun:
Wisdom if you still despise,
  Harder is it to be won.

2 Hasten, mercy to implore!
  Stay not for the morrow's sun,
Lest thy season should be o'er
  Ere this evening's stage be run.

3 Hasten, sinner, to return!
  Stay not for the morrow's sun.
Lest thy lamp should fail to burn
  Ere salvation's work is done.

4 Hasten, sinner, to be blest!
  Stay not for the morrow's sun,
Lest perdition thee arrest
  Ere the morrow is begun.

280 C. M. M. E. H. 369.

Come, humble sinner, in whose breast
  A thousand thoughts revolve,
Come, with your guilt and fear oppressed,
  And make this last resolve:—

2 I'll go to Jesus, though my sin
  Like mountains round me close;
I know his courts, I'll enter in,
  Whatever may oppose.

3 Prostrate I'll lie before his throne,
  And there my guilt confess;
I'll tell him, I'm a wretch undone
  Without his sovereign grace.

4 Perhaps he will admit my plea,
  Perhaps will hear my prayer;
But, if I perish, I will pray,
  And perish only there.

5 I can but perish if I go;
  I am resolved to try:
For if I stay away, I know
  I must forever die.

281 S. M. M. E. H. 359.

Come, weary sinners, come,
  Groaning beneath your load;
The Saviour calls his wanderers home;
  Haste to your pardoning God.

2 Come, all by guilt oppressed,
  Answer the Saviour's call,
"O come, and I will give you rest,
  And I will save you all."

3 Redeemer, full of love,
  We would thy word obey,
And all thy faithful mercies prove
  O take our guilt away.

4 We would on thee rely,
  On thee would cast our care;
Now to thine arms of mercy fly,
  And find salvation there.

282   H.M.   M. E. M. 331.

Blow ye the trumpet, blow,
  The gladly-solemn sound!
Let all the nations know,
  To earth's remotest bound,
The year of jubilee is come!
Return, ye ransomed sinners, home.

2 Jesus, our great High Priest,
  Hath full atonement made:
Ye weary spirits, rest;
  Ye mournful souls, be glad.
The year of jubilee is come!
Return, ye ransomed sinners, home.

3 Extol the Lamb of God,
  The all-atoning Lamb;
Redemption in his blood
  Throughout the world proclaim:
The year of jubilee is come!
Return, ye ransomed sinners, home.

4 Ye slaves of sin and hell,
  Your liberty receive,
And safe in Jesus dwell,
  And blest in Jesus live:
The year of jubilee is come!
Return, ye ransomed sinners, home.

5 Ye who have sold for naught
  Your heritage above,
Shall have it back unbought,
  The gift of Jesus' love:
The year of jubilee is come!
Return, ye ransomed sinners, home.

6 The gospel trumpet hear,
  The news of heavenly grace:
And, saved from earth, appear
  Before your Saviour's face:
The year of jubilee is come!
Return, ye ransomed sinners, home.

283   L.M.   M. R. H. 364.

Come, sinners, to the gospel feast;
Let every soul be Jesus' guest:
Ye need not one be left behind,
For God hath bidden all mankind.

2 Sent by my Lord, on you I call;
The invitation is to all:
Come, all the world! come, sinner, thou!
All things in Christ are ready now.

3 Come, all ye souls by sin oppressed,
Ye restless wanderer after rest;
Ye poor, and maimed, and halt, and blind,
In Christ a hearty welcome find.

4 My message as from God receive;
Ye all may come to Christ and live:
O let his love your hearts constrain,
Nor suffer him to die in vain.

5 See him set forth before your eyes,
  That precious, bleeding sacrifice:
His offered benefits embrace,
  And freely now be saved by grace.

284   L.M.   M. E. H. 390

Stay, thou insulted Spirit, stay,
  Though I have done thee such despite
Nor cast the sinner quite away,
  Nor take thine everlasting flight.

2 Though I have steeled my stubborn heart,
  And shaken off my guilty fears;
And vexed, and urged thee to depart,
  For many long, rebellious years:

3 Though I have most unfaithful been,
  Of all who e'er thy grace received;
Ten thousand times thy goodness seen;
  Ten thousand times thy goodness grieved:

4 Yet, O, the chief of sinners spare,
  In honor of my great High Priest;
Nor in thy righteous anger swear
  To exclude me from thy people's rest.

285   11s.   M E. H. 336.

Delay not, delay not, O sinner, draw near,
  The waters of life are now flowing for thee;
No price is demanded, the Saviour is here,
  Redemption is purchased, salvation is free.

2 Delay not, delay not, why longer abuse
  The love and compassion of Jesus, thy God?
A fountain is open, how canst thou refuse
  To wash and be cleansed in his pardoning blood?

3 Delay not, delay not, O sinner, to come,
  For Mercy still lingers and calls thee to-day;
Her voice is not heard in the vale of the tomb;
  Her message, unheeded, will soon pass away.

4 Delay not, delay not, the Spirit of grace,
  Long grieved and resisted, may take his sad flight,
And leave thee in darkness to finish thy race,
  To sink in the gloom of eternity's night.

5 Delay not, delay not, the hour is at hand,
  The heavens shall fade,
The earth shall dissolve, and the dead, small and great, in the judgment shall stand;
  What power then, O sinner, will lend thee its aid?

286   S. M.   M. E. H. 402.

Ah! whither should I go,
  Burdened, and sick, and faint;
To whom should I my trouble show,
  And pour out my complaint?

2 My Saviour bids me come;
  Ah! why do I delay?
He calls the weary sinner home,
  And yet from him I stay.

3 What is it keeps me back,
  From which I cannot part,
Which will not let the Saviour take
  Possession of my heart?

4 Searcher of hearts, in mine
  Thy trying power display;
Into its darkest corners shine,
  And take the veil away.

287   L. M.   M. E. H. 396.

O for a glance of heavenly day,
  To take this stubborn heart away,
And thaw, with beams of love divine,
This heart, this frozen heart of mine!

2 The rocks can rend; the earth can quake;
The seas can roar; the mountains shake,
Of feeling, all things show some sign,
But this unfeeling heart of mine.

3 To hear the sorrows thou hast felt,
  O Lord, an adamant would melt:
But I can read each moving line,
And nothing moves this heart of mine.

4 Thy judgments, too, which devils fear—
Amazing thought!—unmoved I hear;
Goodness and wrath in vain combine
To stir this stupid heart of mine.

5 But power divine can do the deed;
And, Lord, that power I greatly need;
Thy Spirit can from dross refine,
And melt and change this heart of mine.

288   L. M.   M. E. H. 352.

God calling yet! shall I not hear?
  Earth's pleasure shall I still hold dear?
Shall life's swift passing years all fly,
And still my soul in slumber lie?

2 God calling yet! shall I not rise?
Can I his loving voice despise,
And basely his kind care repay?
He calls me still; can I delay?

3 God calling yet! and shall he knock,
And I my heart the closer lock?
He still is waiting to receive,
And shall I dare his Spirit grieve?

4 God calling yet! and shall I give
No heed, but still in bondage live?
I wait, but he does not forsake;
He calls me still; my heart, awake!

5 God calling yet! I cannot stay;
My heart I yeild without delay:
Vain world, farewell, from thee I part;
The voice of God hath reached my heart.

289   8, 5.   M. B. H. 376.

In the silent midnight watches,
  List,—thy bosom door!
How it knocketh, knocketh, knocketh,
  Knocketh evermore!
Say not 'tis thy pulse is beating:
  'Tis thy heart of sin;
'Tis thy Saviour knocks, and crieth,
  Rise, and let me in!

2 Death comes down with reckless foot-
  To the hall and hut: [step,
Think you death will stand a-knocking
  Where the door is shut?
Jesus waiteth, waiteth, waiteth;
  But thy door is fast!
Grieved, away thy Saviour goeth:
  Death breaks in at last.

3 Then 'tis thine to stand entreating,
  Christ to let thee in;
At the gate of heaven beating,
  Wailing for thy sin.
Nay, alas! thou foolish virgin,
  Hast thou then forgot?
Jesus waited long to know thee,
  But he knows thee not.

290   S. M.   M. E. H. 502.

O come, and dwell in me,
  Spirit of power within,
And bring the glorious liberty
  From sorrow, fear, and sin!

2 The seed of sin's disease
  Spirit of health, remove.
Spirit of finished holiness,
  Spirit of perfect love.

3 Hasten the joyful day
  Which shall my sins consume;
When old things shall be done away
  And all things new become.

4 I want the witness, Lord,
  That all I do is right,
According to thy will and word,
  Well pleasing in thy sight.

5 I ask no higher state;
  Indulge me but in this,
And soon or later then translate
  To my eternal bliss

291 S. M. M. E. H. 401.

AND can I yet delay,
My little all to give?
To tear my soul from earth away,
For Jesus to receive?

2 Nay, but I yield, I yield;
I can hold out no more:
I sink, by dying love compelled,
And own thee conqueror.

3 Though late, I all forsake;
My friends, my all, resign:
Gracious Redeemer, take, O take,
And seal me ever thine.

4 Come, and posess me whole,
Nor hence again remove;
Settle and fix my wavering soul
With all thy weight of love.

5 My one desire be this,
Thy only love to know;
To seek and taste no other bliss,
No other good below.

6 My life, my portion thou;
Thou all sufficient art:
My hope, my heavenly treasure, now
Enter, and keep my heart.

292 L. M. M. R. H. 391.

SHOW pity, Lord, O Lord, forgive;
Let a repenting rebel live:
Are not thy mercies large and free?
May not a sinner trust in thee?

2 My crimes are great, but don't surpass
The power and glory of thy grace;
Great God, thy nature hath no bound,
So let thy pardoning love be found.

3 O wash my soul from every sin,
And make my guilty conscience clean:
Here on my heart the burden lies,
And past offences pain my eyes.

4 My lips with shame my sins confess,
Against thy law, against thy grace;
Lord, should thy judgments grow severe,
I am condemned, but thou art clear.

5 Should sudden vengeance seize my breath,
I must pronounce thee just, in death;
And if my soul were sent to hell,
Thy righteous law approves it well.

6 Yet save a trembling sinner, Lord,
Whose hope, still hovering round thy word, [there,
Would light on some sweet promise
Some sure support against despair.

293 C. P. M. M. E. H. 377.

AUTHOR of faith, to thee I cry,
To thee, who wouldst not have me die,
But know the truth and live:
Open mine eyes to see thy face;
Work in my heart the saving grace;
The life eternal give.

2 Shut up in unbelief, I groan,
And blindly serve a God unknown,
Till thou the veil remove;
The gift unspeakable impart,
And write thy name upon my heart,
And manifest thy love.

3 I know the work is only thine,
The gift of faith is all divine;
But, if on thee we call,
Thou wilt that gracious gift bestow,
And cause our hearts to feel and know
That thou hast died for all.

4 Thou bidd'st us knock and enter in,
Come unto thee, and rest from sin,
The blessing seek and find:
Thou bidd'st us ask thy grace, and have:
Thou canst, thou wouldst, this moment
Both me and all mankind. [save

5 Be it according to thy word;
Now let me find my pardoning Lord;
Let what I ask be given:
The bar of unbelief remove;
Open the door of faith and love,
And take me into heaven.

294 L. M. M. R. H. 418.

Lord, how secure and blest are they
Who feel the joys of pardoned sin!
Should storms of wrath shake earth and sea, [within.
Their minds have heaven and peace

2 The day glides sweetly o'er their heads,
Made up of innocence and love;
And soft and silent as the shades,
Their nightly minutes gently move.

3 Quick as their thoughts their joys come on,
But fly not half so swift away:
Their souls are ever bright as noon,
And calm as summer evenings be.

4 How oft they look to heavenly hills,
Where groves of living pleasure grow;
And longing hopes and cheerful smiles,
Sit undisturbed upon their brow!

5 They scorn to seek earth's golden toys,
But spend the day, and share the night,
In numbering o'er the richer joys [light.
That Heaven prepares for their de-

295 L. M. 61. M. E. H. 422.
And can it be that I should gain
  An interest in the Saviour's blood?
Died he for me, who caused his pain?
  For me, who him to death pursued?
Amazing love! how can it be
That thou, my Lord, shouldst die for me?

2 'Tis mystery all! the immortal dies!
  Who can explore his strange design?
In vain the first-born seraph tries
  To sound the depths of love divine;
'Tis mercy all! let earth adore:
Let angel minds inquire no more.

3 He left his Father's throne above,—
  So free, so infinite his grace!—
Emptied himself of all but love,
  And bled for Adam's helpless race:
'Tis mercy all, immense and free,
  For, O my God, it found out me!

4 Long my imprisoned spir't lay,
  Fast bound in sin and nature's night;
Thine eye diffused a quickening ray,
  I woke, the dungeon flamed with light:
My chains fell off, my heart was free,
I rose, went forth, and followed thee.

5 No condemnation now I dread,
  Jesus, with all in him, is mine;
Alive in him, my living Head,
  And clothed in righteousness divine,
Bold I approach the eternal throne,
And claim the crown, through Christ
  my own.

296 C. M. M. E. H. 405.
Father, I stretch my hands to thee;
  No other help I know:
If thou withdraw thyself from me,
  Ah! whither shall I go!

2 What did thine only Son endure,
  Before I drew my breath?
What pain, what labor, to secure
  My soul from endless death!

3 O Jesus, could I this believe,
  I now should feel thy power;
And all my wants thou wouldst relieve,
  In this accepted hour.

4 Author of faith! to thee I lift
  My weary, longing eyes:
O let me now receive that gift;
  My soul without it dies.

5 Surely thou canst not let me die,
  O speak, and I shall live;
And here I will unwearied lie,
  Till thou thy Spirit give.

6 How would my fainting soul rejoice
  Could I but see thy face!
Now let me hear thy quickening voice,
  And taste thy pardoning grace.

297 C. M. d. M. E. H. 427.
Amazing grace! how sweet the sound,
  That saved a wretch like me!
I once was lost, but now am found,
  Was blind, but now I see.
'Twas grace that taught my heart to fear,
  And grace my fears relieved;
How precious did that grace appear
  The hour I first believed!

2 Through many dangers, toils, and snares,
  I have already come:
'Tis grace hath brought me safe thus far,
  And grace will lead me home.
The Lord has promised good to me,
  His word my hope secures;
He will my shield and portion be
  As long as life endures.

3 Yes, when this flesh and heart shall fail,
  And mortal life shall cease,
I shall possess. within the veil,
  A life of joy and peace.
The earth shall soon dissolve like snow,
  The sun forebear to shine;
But God, who called me here below,
  Will be forever mine.

298 L. M. M. E. H. 447.
O happy day that fixed my choice
  On thee, my Saviour and my God!
Well may this glowing heart rejoice,
  And tell its raptures all abroad.

2 O happy bond, that seals my vows
  To him who merits all my love!
Let cheerful anthems fill his house,
  While to that sacred shrine I move.

3 'Tis done, the great transaction's done;
  I am my Lord's, and he is mine;
He drew me, and I followed on,
  Charmed to confess the voice divine.

4 Now rest, my long-divided heart;
  Fixed on this blissful center, rest;
Nor ever from thy Lord depart,
  With him of every good possessed.

5 High Heaven, that heard the solemn vow,
  That vow renewed shall daily hear,
Till in life's latest hour I bow,
  And bless in death a bond so dear.

299 C. M. M. E. H. 513.

Lord, I believe a rest remains
 To all thy people known;
A rest where pure enjoyment reigns,
 And thou art loved alone:

2 A rest where all our soul's desire
 Is fixed on things above;
Where fear, and sin, and grief, expire,
 Cast out by perfect love.

3 O that I now the rest might know,
 Believe, and enter in!
Now, Saviour, now the power bestow,
 And let me cease from sin.

4 Remove this hardness from my heart;
 This unbelief remove:
To me the rest of faith impart,
 The Sabbath of thy love.

300 10, 11. M. E. H. 453.

O what shall I do my Saviour to praise,
So faithful and true, so plenteous in grace,
So strong to deliver, so good to redeem
The weakest believer that hangs upon him!

2 How happy the man whose heart is set free,
The people that can be joyful in thee!
Their joy is to walk in the light of thy face, [grace;
And still they are talking of Jesus'

3 For thou art their boast, their glory, and power,
And I also trust to see the glad hour,
My soul's new creation, a life from the dead. [head.
The day of salvation that lifts up my

4 For Jesus, my Lord, is now my defense; [from thence;
I trust in his word; none plucks me
Since I have found favor, he all things will do; [anew.
My King and my Saviour shall make me

5 Yes, Lord, I shall see the bliss of thine own; [known;
Thy secret to me shall soon be made
For sorrow and sadness I joy shall receive, [lieve.
And share in the gladness of all that be-

301 L. M. M. E. H. 450.

Jesus, my all, to heaven is gone,
He whom I fix my hopes upon;
His track I see, and I'll pursue
The narrow way, till him I view.

2 The way the holy prophets went,
The road that leads from banishment,
The King's highway of holiness,
I'll go, for all his paths are peace.

3 This is the way I long have sought,
And mourned because I found it not;
My grief a burden long has been,
Because I was not saved from sin.

4 The more I strove against its power,
I felt its weight and guilt the more;
Till late I heard my Saviour say,
"Come hither, soul, I am the way."

5 Lo! glad I come; and thou, blest Lamb,
Shalt take me to thee, as I am;
Nothing but sin have I to give;
Nothing but love shall I receive.

6 Then will I tell to sinners round,
What a dear Saviour I have found;
I'll point to thy redeeming blood,
And say, "behold the way to God."

302 8, 7. d. M. E. H. 491.

Love divine, all love excelling,
 Joy of heaven, to earth come down!
Fix in us thy humble dwelling;
 All thy faithful mercies crown.
Jesus, thou art all compassion,
 Pure, unbounded love thou art;
Visit us with thy salvation;
 Enter every trembling heart.

2 Breathe, O breathe thy loving Spirit
 Into every troubled breast!
Let us all in thee inherit,
 Let us find that second rest.
Take away our bent to sinning;
 Alpha and Omega be;
End of faith, as its begining,
 Set our hearts at liberty.

3 Come, almighty to deliver,
 Let us all thy life receive;
Suddenly return, and never,
 Nevermore thy temples leave:
Thee we would be always blessing,
 Serve thee as thy hosts above,
Pray, and praise thee without cease
 Glory in thy perfect love.

4 Finish then thy new creation;
 Pure and spotless let us be;
Let us see thy great salvation,
 Perfectly restored in thee:
Changed from glory into glory,
 Till in heaven we take our place,
Till we cast our crowns before thee,
 Lost in wonder, love, and praise.

303 7, 6, 8. M. E. H. 456.

VAIN, delusive world, adieu,
  With all of creature good!
Only Jesus I pursue.
  Who bought me with his blood:
All thy pleasures I forego;
  I trample on thy wealth and pride;
Only Jesus will I know,
  And Jesus crucified.

2 Other knowledge I disdain;
  'Tis all but vanity:
Christ, the Lamb of God, was slain,
  He tasted death for me.
Me to save from endless woe
  The sin-atoning Victim died:
Only Jesus will I know,
  And Jesus crucified.

3 Here will I set up my rest;
  My fluctuating heart
From the haven of his breast
  Shall never more depart:
Whither should a sinner go?
  His wounds for me stand open wide;
Only Jesus will I know,
  And Jesus crucified.

4 Him to know is life and peace,
  And pleasure without end;
This is all my happiness,
  On Jesus to depend;
Daily in his grace to grow,
  And ever in his faith abide;
Only Jesus will I know,
  And Jesus crucified.

304 8, 7, 4. M. E. H. 340.

COME, ye sinners, poor and needy,
  Weak and wounded, sick and sore;
Jesus ready stands to save you,
  Full of pity, love, and power:
    He is able,
  He is willing: doubt no more.

2 Now, ye needy, come and welcome;
  God's free bounty glorify;
True belief and true repentance,
  Every grace that brings you nigh,
    Without money,
  Come to Jesus Christ and buy.

3 Let not conscience make you linger,
  Nor of fitness fondly dream;
All the fitness he requireth
  Is to feel your need of him:
    This he gives you:
  'Tis the Spirit's glimmering beam.

4 Come, ye weary, heavy-laden,
  Bruised and mangled by the fall;

If you tarry till you're better,
  You will never come at all;
    Not the righteous,—
  Sinners Jesus came to call.

5 Agonizing in the garden,
  Your Redeemer prostrate lies;
On the bloody tree behold him!
  Hear him cry, before he dies,
    "It is finished!"
  Sinners, will not this suffice?

305 C. M. M. E. H. 666.

MUST Jesus bear the cross alone,
  And all the world go free?
No, there's a cross for every one,
  And there's a cross for me.

2 How happy are the saints above,
  Who once went sorrowing here!
But now they taste unmingled love,
  And joy without a tear.

3 The consecrated cross I'll bear,
  Till death shall set me free,
And then go home my crown to wear,
  For there's a crown for me.

306 H. M. M. E. H. 438.

ARISE, my soul, arise;
  Shake off thy guilty fears:
The bleeding Sacrifice
  In my behalf appears:
Before the throne my Surety stands,
My name is written on his hands.

2 He ever lives above,
  For me to intercede;
His all-redeeming love,
  His precious blood to plead:
His blood atoned for all our race,
And sprinkles now the throne of grace.

3 Five bleeding wounds he bears,
  Received on Calvary;
They pour effectual prayers,
  They strongly plead for me:
"Forgive him, O forgive," they cry,
"Nor let that ransomed sinner die."

4 The Father hears him pray,
  His dear anointed One:
He cannot turn away
  The presence of his Son:
His Spirit answers to the blood,
And tells me I am born of God.

5 My God is reconciled;
  His pardoning voice I hear:
He owns me for his child;
  I can no longer fear:
With confidence I now draw nigh,
And, "Father, Abba, Father," cry.

307   L. M.   M. E. H. 461.

I THIRST, thou wounded Lamb of God,
To wash me in thy cleansing blood;
To dwell within thy wounds; then pain
Is sweet, and life or death is gain.

2 Take my poor heart, and let it be
Forever closed to all but thee;
Seal thou my breast, and let me wear
That pledge of love forever there.

3 How blest are they who still abide
Close sheltered in thy bleeding side!
Who thence their life and strength derive,
And by thee move, and in thee live.

4 What are our works but sin and death,
Till thou thy quickening Spirit breathe?
Thou giv'st the power thy grace to move;
O wondrous grace! O boundless love!

5 How can it be, thou heavenly King,
That thou shouldst us to glory bring?
Make slaves the partners of thy throne,
Decked with a never-fading crown!

6 Hence our hearts melt, our eyes o'erflow,
Our words are lost, nor will we know,
Nor will we think of aught beside,
"My Lord, my Love is crucified."

308   H. M.   M. E. H. 493.

YE ransomed sinners, hear,
  The prisoners of the Lord;
And wait till Christ appear,
  According to his word:
Rejoice in hope, rejoice with me,
We shall from all our sins be free.

2 In God we put our trust;
  If we our sins confess,
Faithful is he and just,
  From all unrighteousness
To cleanse us all, both you and me:
We shall from all our sins be free.

3 Who Jesus' sufferings share,
  My fellow-prisoners now,
Ye soon the crown shall wear
  On your triumphant brow:
Rejoice in hope, rejoice with me,
We shall from all our sins be free.

4 The word of God is sure,
  And never can remove;
We shall in heart be pure,
  And perfected in love;
Rejoice in hope, rejoice with me,
We shall from all our sins be free.

5 Then let us gladly bring
  Our sacrifice of praise:
Let us give thanks and sing,
  And glory in his grace:
Rejoice in hope, rejoice with me,
We shall from all our sins be free.

309   C. M.   M. E. H. 593.

AM I a soldier of the cross,
  A follower of the Lamb,
And shall I fear to own his cause,
  Or blush to speak his name?

2 Must I be carried to the skies
  On flowery beds of ease,
While others fought to win the prize
  And sailed through bloody seas?

3 Are there no foes for me to face?
  Must I not stem the flood?
Is this vile world a friend to grace,
  To help me on to God?

4 Sure I must fight, if I would reign;
  Increase my courage, Lord;
I'll bear the toil, endure the pain,
  Supported by thy word.

5 Thy saints in all this glorious war
  Shall conquer, though they die:
They see the triumph from afar,
  By faith they bring it nigh.

6 When that illustrious day shall rise,
  And all thy armies shine
In robes of victory through the skies,
  The glory shall be thine.

310   L. M.   M. E. H. 465.

LORD, I am thine, entirely thine,
Purchased and saved by blood divine;
With full consent thine I would be,
And own thy sovereign right in me.

2 Grant one poor sinner more a place
Among the children of thy grace;
A wretched sinner, lost to God,
But ransomed by Immanuel's blood.

3 Thine would I live, thine would I die,
Be thine through all eternity;
The vow is past beyond repeal,
And now I set the solemn seal.

4 Here, at that cross where flows the blood
That bought my guilty soul for God,
Thee my new Master now I call,
And consecrate to thee my all.

5 Do thou assist a feeble worm
The great engagement to perform;
Thy grace can full assistance lend,
And on that grace I dare depend.

311 L. M. M r. 11. 495.

O THAT my load of sin were gone!
  O that I could at last submit
At Jesus' feet to lay it down—
  To lay my soul at Jesus' feet!

2 Rest for my soul I long to find:
  Saviour of all, if mine thou art,
Give me thy meek and lowly mind,
  And stamp thine image on my heart.

3 Break off the yoke of inbred sin,
  And fully set my spirit free;
I cannot rest till pure within,
  Till I am wholly lost in thee.

4 Fain would I learn of thee, my God,
  Thy light and easy burden prove,
The cross all stained with hallowed
  The labor of thy dying love. [blood

5 I would, but thou must give the
    power;
  My heart from every sin release;
Bring near, bring near the joyful hour,
  And fill me with thy perfect peace.

312 C. M. M R. H. 667.

O FOR a faith that will not shrink,
  Though pressed by every foe,
That will not tremble on the brink
  Of any earthly woe!

2 That will not murmur nor complain
  Beneath the chastening rod,
But, in the hour of grief or pain,
  Will lean upon its God:

3 A faith that shines more bright and
  When tempests rage without; [clear
That when in danger knows no fear,
  In darkness feels no doubt;

4 That bears unmoved the world's
    dread frown,
  Nor heeds its scornful smile;
That seas of trouble cannot drown,
  Nor Satan's arts beguile;

5 A faith that keeps the narrow way
  Till life's last hour is fled,
And with a pure and heavenly ray
  Illumes a dying bed.

6 Lord, give us such a faith as this,
  And then, whate'er may come,
We'll taste, e'en here, the hallowed bliss
  Of an eternal home.

313 C. M. M. R. H. 518.

JESUS, thine all-victorious love
  Shed in my heart abroad:
Then shall my feet no longer rove,
  Rooted and fixed in God.

2 O that in me the sacred fire
  Might now begin to glow,
Burn up the dross of base desire,
  And make the mountains flow!

3 O that it now from heaven might fall,
  And all my sins consume!
Come, Holy Ghost, for thee I call;
  Spirit of burning, come!

4 Refining fire, go through my heart;
  Illuminate my soul;
Scatter thy life through every part,
  And sanctify the whole.

5 My steadfast soul, from falling free,
  Shall then no longer move,
While Christ is all the world to me,
  And all my heart is love.

314 C. M. M R. H. 533.

FOREVER here my rest shall be,
  Close to thy bleeding side;
This all my hope, and all my plea,
  "For me the Saviour died."

2 My dying Saviour and my God,
  Fountain for guilt and sin,
Sprinkle me ever with thy blood,
  And cleanse and keep me clean.

3 Wash me and make me thus thine
  Wash me, and mine thou art; [own;
Wash me but not my feet alone,
  My hands, my head, my heart.

4 The atonement of thy blood apply,
  Till faith to sight improve;
Till hope in full fruition die,
  And all my soul be love.

315 C. M. M. R. H. 581.

O FOR a heart to praise my God,
  A heart from sin set free!
A heart that always feels thy blood,
  So freely spilt for me!

2 A heart resigned, submissive, meek,
  My great Redeemer's throne;
Where only Christ is heard to speak,
  Where Jesus reigns alone.

3 O for a lowly, contrite heart,
  Believing, true, and clean,
Which neither life nor death can part
  From him that dwells within!

4 A heart in every thought renewed,
  And full of love divine;
Perfect, and right, and pure, and good,
  A copy, Lord, of thine.

5 Thy nature, gracious Lord, impart;
  Come quickly from above;
Write thy new name upon my heart,
  Thy new, best name of Love.

316 C.P.M. M. E. H. 540.

O LOVE divine, how sweet thou art!
  When shall I find my willing heart
  All taken up by thee?
I thirst, I faint, I die to prove
The greatness of redeeming love,
  The love of Christ to me.

2 Stronger his love than death or hell;
  Its riches are unsearchable;
  The first-born sons of light
Desire in vain its depths to see;
They cannot reach the mystery,
  The length, the breadth, the height.

3 God only knows the love of God;
  O that it now were shed abroad
  In this poor, stony heart!
For love I sigh, for love I pine;
This only port'on, Lord, be mine;
  Be mine this better part.

4 O that I could forever sit
  With Mary at the Master's feet!
  Be this my happy choice;
My only care, delight, and bliss,
My joy, my heaven on earth, be this,
  To hear the Bridegroom's voice.

5 O that I could, with favored John,
  Recline my weary head upon
  The dear Redeemer's breast!
From care and sin and sorrow free,
Give me, O Lord, to find in thee
  My everlasting rest.

317 S. M. M. E. H. 574.

A CHARGE to keep I have,
  A God to glorify;
A never-dying soul to save,
  And fit it for the sky.
To serve the present age,
  My calling to fulfill,
O may it all my powers engage,
  To do my Master's will.

2 Arm me with jealous care,
  As in thy sight to live;
And oh, thy servant, Lord, prepare,
  A strict account to give.
Help me to watch and pray,
  And on thyself rely,
Assured, if I my trust betray,
  I shall forever die.

318 C. M. M. E. H. 594.

AWAKE, my soul, stretch every nerve,
  And press with vigor on;
A heavenly race demands thy zeal,
  And an immortal crown.

2 A cloud of witnesses around
  Hold thee in full survey;
Forget the steps already trod,
  And onward urge thy way.

3 'Tis God's all-animating voice
  That calls thee from on high;
'Tis his own hand presents the prize
  To thine aspiring eye:—

4 That prize, with peerless glories
  Which shall new luster boast, [bright,
When victors' wreaths and monarchs'
  Shall blend in common dust. [gems

5 Blest Saviour, introduced by thee,
  Have I my race begun;
And, crowned with victory, at thy feet
  I'll lay my honors down.

319 C.P.M. M. E. H. 571.

BE it my only wisdom here,
To serve the Lord with filial fear,
  With loving gratitude:
Superior sense may I display,
By shunning every evil way,
  And walking in the good.

2 O may I still from sin depart;
A wise and understanding heart,
  Jesus, to me be given:
And let me through thy Spirit know
To glorify my God below,
  And find my way to heaven.

320 7, 6, 5. M. E. H. 565.

WORK, for the night is coming,
  Work through the morning hours;
Work while the dew is sparkling,
  Work 'mid springing flowers;
Work when the day grows brighter,
  Work in the glowing sun;
Work, for the night is coming,
  When man's work is done.

2 Work, for the night is coming,
  Work through the sunny noon;
Fill brightest hours with labor,
  Rest comes sure and soon.
Give every flying minute
  Something to keep in store:
Work, for the night is coming,
  When man works no more.

3 Work, for the night is coming,
  Under the sunset skies;
While their bright tints are glowing,
  Work, for daylight flies.
Work till the last beam fadeth,
  Fadeth to shine no more;
Work while the night is darkening,
  When man's work is o'er.

321   C. M.   M. E. H. 596.

O it is hard to work for God,
  To rise and take his part
Upon this battle-field of earth,
  And not sometimes lose heart !

2 He hides himself so wondrously,
  As though there were no God ;
He is least seen when all the powers
  Of ill are most abroad ;

3 Or he deserts us in the hour
  The fight is all but lost ;
And seems to leave us to ourselves
  Just when we need him most.

4 It is not so, but so it looks ;
  And we lose courage then ; [kept
And doubts will come if God hath
  His promises to men.

5 But right is right, since God is God;
  And right the day must win ;
To doubt would be disloyalty,
  To falter would be sin !

322   11, 10.   M. E. H. 652.

Come unto me, when shadows darkly
    gather,   [tressed,
When the sad heart is weary and dis-
Seeking for comfort from your heaven-
    ly Father,   [rest.
  Come unto me, and I will give you

2 Large are the mansions in thy Fa-
    ther's dwelling,   [er dim ;
Glad are the homes that sorrows nev-
Sweet are the harps in holy music
    swelling,   [heavenly hymn.
Soft are the tones which raise the

3 There, like an Eden blossoming in
    gladness,   [rudely pressed ;
Bloom the fair flowers the earth too
Come unto me, all ye who droop in
    sadness,   [rest.
  Come unto me, and I will give you

323   L. M.   M. E. H. 602.

It may not be our lot to wield
  The sickle in the ripened field ;
Nor ours to hear, on summer eves,
  The reaper's song among the sheaves.

2 Yet where our duty's task is wrought
  In unison with God's great thought,
The near and future blend in one,
  And whatsoe'er is willed, is done.

3 And ours the grateful service whence
  Comes, day by day, the recompense ;
The hope, the trust, the purpose stayed,
  The fountain, and the noonday shade.

4 And were this life the utmost span,
  The only end and aim of man,
Better the toil of fields like these
  Than waking dream and slothful ease.

5 But life, though falling like our grain,
  Like that revives and springs again ;
And, early called, how blest are they
  Who wait in heaven, their harvest day !

324   L. M.   M. E. H. 605.

My gracious Lord, I own thy right
  To every service I can pay,
And call it my supreme delight
  To hear thy dictates, and obey.

2 What is my being but for thee,
  Its sure support, its noblest end?
'Tis my delight thy face to see,
  And serve the cause of such a Friend

3 I would not sigh for worldly joy,
  Or to increase my worldly good ;
Nor future days nor powers employ
  To spread a sounding name abroad.

4 'Tis to my Saviour I would live,
  To him who for my ransom died ;
Nor could all worldly honor give
  Such bliss as crowns me at his side.

5 His work my hoary age shall bless,
  When youthful vigor is no more ;
And my last hour of life confess
  His dying love, his saving power.

325   C. P. M.   M. E. H. 542.

O glorious hope of perfect love !
  It lifts me up to things above ;
    It bears on eagles' wings ;
It gives my ravished soul a taste,
And makes me for some moments feast
    With Jesus' priests and kings.

2 Rejoicing now in earnest hope,
I stand, and from the mountain top
    See all the land below ;
Rivers of milk and honey rise,
And all the fruits of Paradise
    In endless plenty grow.

3 A land of corn, and wine, and oil,
Favored with God's peculiar smile,
    With every blessing blest ; [ness,
There dwells the Lord, our Righteous-
And keeps his own in perfect peace,
    And everlasting rest.

4 O that I might at once go up ;
No more on this side Jordan stop,
    But now the land possess ;
This moment end my legal years,
Sorrows and sins, and doubts and fears,
    A howling wilderness !

326 L.M.d. M. E. H. 688.

Sweet hour of prayer, sweet hour of prayer,
That calls me from a world of care,
And bids me, at my Father's throne,
Make all my wants and wishes known!
In seasons of distress and grief
My soul has often found relief,
And oft escaped the tempter's snare,
By thy return, sweet hour of prayer.

2 Sweet hour of prayer, sweet hour of prayer,
Thy wings shall my petition bear
To him, whose truth and faithfulness
Engage the waiting soul to bless:
And since he bids me seek his face,
Believe his word, and trust his grace,
I'll cast on him my every care,
And wait for thee, sweet hour of prayer.

3 Sweet hour of prayer, sweet hour of prayer,
May I thy consolation share,
Till, from Mount Pisgah's lofty height,
I view my home, and take my flight:
This robe of flesh I'll drop, and rise,
To seize the everlasting prize;
And shout, while passing through the air, [prayer!
Farewell, farewell, sweet hour of

327 11s. M. E. H. 679.

How firm a foundation, ye saints of the Lord, [word!
Is laid for your faith in his excellent
What more can he say, than to you he hath sa'd, [fled?
To you who for refuge to Jesus have

2 "Fear not, I am with thee, O be not dismayed, [aid;
For I am thy God, I will still give thee
I'll strengthen thee, help thee, and cause thee to stand, [hand.
Upheld by my gracious, omnipotent

3 "When through the deep waters I call thee to go, [flow;
The rivers of sorrow shall not over-
For I will be with thee thy trials to bless, [tress.
And sanctify to thee thy deepest dis-

4 "When through fiery trials thy pathway shall lie, [supply,
My grace, all-sufficient, shall be thy
The flame shall not hurt thee; I only design [to refine.
Thy dross to consume, and thy gold

5 "E'en down to old age all my people shall prove [love;
My sovereign, eternal, unchangeable
And when hoary hairs shall their temples adorn, [be borne.
Like lambs they shall still in my bosom

6 "The soul that on Jesus hath leaned for repose,
I will not, I will not desert to his foes;
That soul, though all hell should endeavor to shake,
I'll never, no never, no never forsake!"

328 6s. M. E. H. 655.

Thy way, not mine, O Lord,
However dark it be!
Lead me by thine own hand;
Choose out the path for me
I dare not choose my lot;
I would not if I might;
Choose thou for me, my God,
So shall I walk aright.

2 The kingdom that I seek
Is thine; so let the way
That leads to it be thine,
Else I must surely stray.
Take thou my cup, and it
With joy or sorrow fill,
As best to thee may seem;
Choose thou my good and ill.

3 Choose thou for me my friends,
My sickness or my health;
Choose thou my cares for me,
My poverty or wealth.
Not mine, not mine the choice,
In things or great or small;
Be thou my guide, my strength,
My wisdom, and my all.

329 C. M. M. E. H. 659.

When I can read my title clear
To mansions in the skies,
I bid farewell to every fear,
And wipe my weeping eyes.

2 Should earth against my soul engage,
And fiery darts be hurled,
Then I can smile at Satan's rage,
And face a frowning world.

3 Let cares like a wild deluge come,
Let storms of sorrow fall,
So I but safely reach my home,
My God, my heaven, my all.

4 There I shall bathe my weary soul
In seas of heavenly rest,
And not a wave of trouble roll
Across my peaceful breast.

330 10, 4, 10. M. E. H. 582.

LEAD, kindly Light, amid the encircling
    Lead thou me on!   [gloom,
The night is dark, and I am far from
    Lead thou me on!   [home;
Keep thou my feet; I do not ask to see
The distant scene; one step enough for
  me.

2 I was not ever thus, nor prayed that
    Shouldst lead me on;   [thou
I loved to choose and see my path; but
    Lead thou me on!   [now
I loved the garish day, and, spite of fears,
Pride ruled my will. Remember not
  past years!

3 So long thy power hath blest me,
    Will lead me on   [sure it still
O'er moor and fen, o'er crag and tor-
    The night is gone,   [rent, till
And with the morn those angel faces
  smile   [awhile!
Which I have loved long since, and lost

331 L. M. M. E. H. 622.

HE leadeth me! O blessed thought!
O words with heavenly comfort fraught!
Whate'er I do, where'er I be,
Still 'tis God's hand that leadeth me.

Cho.—He leadeth me, he leadeth me,
  By his own hand he leadeth me;
  His faithful follower I would be,
  For by his hand he leadeth me.

2 Sometimes 'mid scenes of deepest
  gloom,
Sometimes where Eden's bowers bloom,
By waters still, o'er troubled sea,—
Still 'tis his hand that leadeth me!

3 Lord, I would clasp thy hand in mine,
Nor ever murmur nor repine,
Content, whatever lot I see,
Since 'tis my God that leadeth me!

4 And when my task on earth is done,
When, by thy grace, the victory's won,
E'en death's cold wave I will not flee,
Since God through Jordan leadeth me.

332 C. M. M. E. H. 700.

JESUS, the very thought of thee
  With sweetness fills the breast;
But sweeter far thy face to see,
  And in thy presence rest.

2 No voice can sing, no heart can frame,
  Nor can the memory find
A sweeter sound than Jesus' name,
  The Saviour of mankind.

3 O Hope of every contrite heart,
  O Joy of all the meek,
To those who ask, how kind thou art!
  How good, to those who seek!

4 But what to those who find? Ah, this
  Nor tongue nor pen can show:
The love of Jesus, what it is,
  None but his loved ones know.

5 Jesus, our only joy be thou,
  As thou our prize wilt be;
In thee be all our glory now,
  And through eternity.

333 S. M. M. E. H. 636.

IF, on a quiet sea,
  Toward heaven we calmly sail,
With grateful hearts, O God, to thee,
  We'll own the favoring gale.

2 But, should the surges rise,
  And rest delay to come,
Blest be the tempest, kind the storm,
  Which drives us nearer home.

3 Soon shall our doubts and fears
  All yield to thy control;
Thy tender mercies shall illume
  The midnight of the soul.

4 Teach us, in every state,
  To make thy will our own;
And when the joys of sense depart,
  To live by faith alone.

334 6s. M. E. H. 654.

MY Jesus, as thou wilt:
  O may thy will be mine;
Into thy hand of love
  I would my all resign.
Through sorrow or through joy,
  Conduct me as thine own,
And help me still to say,
  "My Lord, thy will be done."

2 My Jesus, as thou wilt:
  Though seen through many a tear,
Let not my star of hope
  Grow dim or disappear.
Since thou on earth hast wept
  And sorrowed oft alone,
If I must weep with thee,
  My Lord, thy will be done.

3 My Jesus, as thou wilt:
  All shall be well for me;
Each changing future scene
  I gladly trust with thee.
Straight to my home above,
  I travel calmly on,
And sing in life or death,
  "My Lord, thy will be done."

335 C. M. M. E. H. 611.

O thou who driest the mourner's tear,
 How dark this world would be,
If, when deceived and wounded here,
 We could not fly to thee !

2 The friends who in our sunshine live,
 When winter comes are flown ;
And he who has but tears to give,
 Must weep those tears alone.

3 But thou wilt heal that broken heart,
 Which, like the plants that throw
Their fragrance from the wounded part,
 Breathes sweetness out of woe.

4 O, who could bear life's stormy doom,
 Did not thy wing of love   [gloom,
Come brightly wafting through the
 Our peace-branch from above?

5 Then sorrow, touched by thee, grows
 With more than rapture's ray; [bright
As darkness shows us worlds of light
 We never saw by day.

336 8, 7, 4.   M. E. H. 646.

Gently, Lord, O gently lead us
 Through this gloomy vale of tears;
And, O Lord, in mercy give us
 Thy rich grace in all our fears,
  O refresh us,
 Traveling through this wilderness.

2 When temptation's darts assail us,
 When in devious paths we stray,
Let thy goodness never fail us,
 Lead us in thy perfect way.

3 In the hour of pain and anguish,
 In the hour when death draws near,
Suffer not our hearts to languish,
 Suffer not our souls to fear.

4 When this mortal life is ended,
 Bid us in thine arms to rest,
Till, by angel-bands attended,
 We awake among the blest.

337 C. M.   M. E. H. 704.

My God, the spring of all my joys,
 The life of my delight,
The glory of my brightest days,
 And comfort of my nights !

2 In darkest shades, if thou appear,
 My dawning is begun ;   [star,
Thou art my soul's bright morning
 And thou my rising sun.

3 The opening heavens around me
 With beams of sacred bliss, [shine
If Jesus shows his mercy mine,
 And whispers I am his.

4 My soul would leave this heavy clay
 At that transporting word,
Run up with joy the shining way,
 To see and praise my Lord.

5 Fearless of hell and ghastly death,
 I'd break through every foe ;
The wings of love and arms of faith
 Would bear me conqueror through.

338 S. M.   M. E. H. 673.

Give to the winds thy fears ;
 Hope, and be undismayed ; [tears;
God hears thy sighs and counts thy
 God shall lift up thy head.

2 Through waves, and clouds, and
 He gently clears thy way ; [storms,
Wait thou his time, so shall this night
 Soon end in joyous day.

3 Still heavy is thy heart?
 Still sink thy spirits down ?
Cast off the weight, let fear depart,
 And every care be gone.

4 What though thou rulest not ?
 Yet heaven, and earth, and hell
Proclaim, "God sitteth on the throne,
 And ruleth all things well."

5 Leave to his sovereign sway
 To choose and to command : [way,
So shalt thou, wondering, own his
 How wise, how strong his hand !

6 Far, far above thy thought
 His counsel shall appear,
When fully he the work hath wrought
 That caused thy needless fear.

339 8, 7, 4.   M. E. H. 768.

Zion stands with hills surrounded,
 Zion, kept by power divine :
All her foes shall be confounded,
 Though the world in arms combine :
  Happy Zion,
 What a favored lot is thine !

2 Every human tie may perish ;
 Friend to friend unfaithful prove ;
Mothers cease their own to cherish ;
 Heaven and earth at last remove ;
  But no changes
 Can attend Jehovah's love.

3 In the furnace God may prove thee,
 Thence to bring thee forth more bright,
But can never cease to love thee ;
 Thou art precious in his sight :
  God is with thee,
 God, thine everlasting light.

340 C. M. M. E. H. 707.

There is an eye that never sleeps
  Beneath the wing of night;
There is an ear that never shuts,
  When sink the beams of light.

2 There is an arm that never tires,
  When human strength gives way;
There is a love that never fails,
  When earthly loves decay.

3 That eye is fixed on seraph throngs;
  That arm upholds the sky;
That ear is filled with angel songs;
  That love is throned on high.

4 But there's a power which man can
  When mortal aid is vain, [wield,
That eye, that arm, that love to reach,
  That listening ear to gain.

5 That power is prayer which soars on
  Through Jesus, to the throne, [high,
And moves the hand which moves the
  To bring salvation down. [world,

341 C. M. M. E. H. 710.

Prayer is the soul's sincere desire,
  Uttered or unexpressed;
The motion of a hidden fire
  That trembles in the breast.

2 Prayer is the burden of a sigh,
  The falling of a tear,
The upward glancing of an eye,
  When none but God is near.

3 Prayer is the simplest form of speech
  That infant lips can try;
Prayer the sublimest strains that reach
  The Majesty on high.

4 Prayer is the contrite sinner's voice,
  Returning from his ways;
While angels in their songs rejoice,
  And cry, "Behold, he prays!"

5 Prayer is the Christian's vital breath,
  The Christian's native air,
His watchword at the gates of death;
  He enters heaven with prayer.

6 O thou, by whom we come to God,
  The Life, the Truth, the Way;
The path of prayer thyself hast trod:
  Lord, teach us how to pray!

342 L. M. 6l. M. E. H. 737.

Come, O thou Traveler unknown,
  Whom still I hold but cannot see;
My company before is gone,
  And I am left alone with thee:
With thee all night I mean to stay,
And wrestle till the break of day.

2 I need not tell thee who I am,
  My sin and misery declare;
Thyself hast called me by my name,
  Look on thy hands, and read it there.
But who, I ask thee, who art thou?
Tell me thy name, and tell me now.

3 In vain thou strugglest to get free,
  I never will unloose my hold:
Art thou the Man that died for me?
  The secret of thy love unfold:
Wrestling, I will not let thee go,
Till I thy name, thy nature know.

4 Wilt thou not yet to me reveal
  Thy new, unutterable name?
Tell me, I still beseech thee, tell;
  To know it now resolved I am:
Wrestling, I will not let thee go,
Till I thy name, thy nature know.

5 What though my shrinking flesh
    complain,
  And murmur to contend so long?
I rise superior to my pain;
  When I am weak, then I am strong·
And when my all of strength shall fail,
I shall with the God-man prevail.

343 6, 4. M. E. H. 762.

My faith looks up to thee,
Thou Lamb of Calvary,
  Saviour divine:
Now hear me while I pray,
Take all my guilt away,
O let me from this day
  Be wholly thine.

2 May thy rich grace impart
Strength to my aching heart,
  My zeal inspire;
As thou hast died for me,
O may my love to thee
Pure, warm, and changeless be,—
  A living fire.

3 While life's dark maze I tread,
And griefs around me spread,
  Be thou my guide;
Bid darkness turn to day,
Wipe sorrow's tears away,
Nor let me ever stray
  From thee aside.

4 When ends life's transient dream,
When death's cold, sullen stream
  Shall o'er me roll;
Blest Saviour, then, in love,
Fear and distrust remove;
O bear me safe above,—
  A ransomed soul.

CONGREGATIONAL.

344 C. M. M. E. H. 712.

Talk with us, Lord, thyself reveal,
  While here o'er earth we rove;
Speak to our hearts, and let us feel
  The kindling of thy love.

2 With thee conversing, we forget
  All time, and toil, and care;
Labor is rest, and pain is sweet,
  If thou, my God, art here.

3 Here, then, my God, vouchsafe to stay,
  And bid my heart rejoice;
My bounding heart shall own thy sway,
  And echo to thy voice.

4 Thou callest me to seek thy face,—
  'Tis all I wish to seek;
To attend the whispers of thy grace,
  And hear thee inly speak.

5 Let this my every hour employ
  Till I thy glory see;
Enter into my Master's joy,
  And find my heaven in thee.

345 7s. M. E. H. 720.

Children of the heavenly King,
As we journey let us sing;
Sing our Saviour's worthy praise,
Glorious in his works and ways.

2 We are traveling home to God,
In the way our father's trod;
They are happy now, and we
Soon their happiness shall see.

3 O ye banished seed, be glad;
Christ our Advocate is made:
Us to save our flesh assumes,
Brother to our souls becomes.

4 Lift your eyes, ye sons of light;
Zion's city is in sight;
There our endless home shall be,
There our Lord we soon shall see.

5 Fear not, brethren, joyful stand
On the borders of our land;
Jesus Christ, our Father's Son,
Bids us undismayed go on.

6 Lord, obediently we'll go,
Gladly leaving all below:
Only thou our Leader be,
And we still will follow thee.

346 S. M. M. E. H. 751.

My God, my Life, my Love,
  To thee, to thee I call;
I cannot live if thou remove,
  For thou art all in all.

2 Thy shining grace can cheer
  This dungeon where I dwell;

'Tis paradise when thou art here;
  If thou depart, 'tis hell.

3 The smilings of thy face,
  How amiable they are!
'Tis heaven to rest in thine embrace,
  And nowhere else but there.

4 Not all the harps above
  Can make a heavenly place,
If God his residence remove,
  Or but conceal his face.

5 Thou art the sea of love,
  Where all my pleasures roll:
The circle where my passions move,
  And center of my soul.

347 S. M. M. E. H. 773.

O Lord, thy work revive,
  In Zion's gloomy hour,
And let our dying graces live
  By thy restoring power.

2 O let thy chosen few
  Awake to earnest prayer;
Their covenant again renew,
  And walk in filial fear.

3 Thy Spirit then will speak
  Through lips of humble clay,
Till hearts of adamant shall break,
  Till rebels shall obey.

4 Now lend thy gracious ear;
  Now listen to our cry:
O come, and bring salvation near;
  Our souls on thee rely.

348 6, 4, 6. M. E. H. 729.

More love to thee, O Christ,
  More love to thee!
Hear thou the prayer I make,
  On bended knee;
This is my earnest plea,
More love, O Christ, to thee,
  More love to thee!

2 Once earthly joy I craved,
  Sought peace and rest;
Now thee alone I seek,
  Give what is best:
This all my prayer shall be,
More love, O Christ, to thee,
  More love to thee!

3 Then shall my latest breath
  Whisper thy praise;
This be the parting cry
  My heart shall raise,
This still its prayer shall be,
More love, O Christ, to thee,
  More love to thee!

Emory Hymnal—Q

349 S. M. M. E. H. 770.

I love thy kingdom, Lord,
 The house of thine abode,
The Church our blest Redeemer saved
 With his own precious blood.

2 I love thy Church, O God!
 Her walls before thee stand,
Dear as the apple of thine eye,
 And graven on thy hand.

3 For her my tears shall fall,
 For her my prayers ascend;
To her my cares and toils be given,
 Till toils and cares shall end.

4 Beyond my highest joy
 I prize her heavenly ways,
Her sweet communion, solemn vows,
 Her hymns of love and praise.

5 Sure as thy truth shall last,
 To Zion shall be given
The brightest glories earth can yield,
 And brighter bliss of heaven.

350 C. M. M. E. H. 784.

Try us, O God, and search the ground
 Of every sinful heart;
Whate'er of sin in us is found,
 O bid it all depart.

2 If to the right or left we stray,
 Leave us not comfortless;
But guide our feet into the way
 Of everlasting peace.

3 Help us to help each other, Lord,
 Each other's cross to bear;
Let each his friendly aid afford,
 And feel his brother's care.

4 Help us to build each other up,
 Our little stock improve;
Increase our faith, confirm our hope,
 And perfect us in love.

5 Up into thee, our living Head,
 Let us in all things grow,
Till thou hast made us free indeed,
 And spotless here below.

6 Then, when the mighty work is
 Receive thy ready bride: [wrought,
Give us in heaven a happy lot
 With all the sanctified.

351 8,7,4. or 8,7. d. M. E. H. 733.

O thou God of my salvation,
 My Redeemer from all sin;
Moved by thy divine compassion,
 Who hast died my heart to win,
  I will praise thee;
 Where shall I thy praise begin?

2 Though unseen, I love the Saviour;
 He hath brought salvation near;
Manifests his pardoning favor;
 And when Jesus doth appear,
  Soul and body
 Shall his glorious image bear.

3 While the angel choirs are crying,
 "Glory to the great I AM,"
I with them will still be vying—
 Glory! glory to the Lamb!
  O how precious
 Is the sound of Jesus' name!

4 Angels now are hovering round us,
 Unperceived amid the throng;
Wondering at the love that crowned
 Glad to join the holy song: [us,
  Hallelujah,
 Love and praise to Christ belong!

352 6,4,6. M. E. H. 724.

Nearer, my God, to thee!
 Nearer to thee,
E'en though it be a cross
 That raiseth me;
Still all my song shall be,
 Nearer, my God, to thee,
  Nearer to thee!

2 Though like the wanderer,
 The sun gone down,
Darkness be over me,
 My rest a stone,
Yet in my dreams I'd be
 Nearer, my God, to thee,
  Nearer to thee!

3 There let the way appear,
 Steps unto heaven;
All that thou sendest me,
 In mercy given;
Angels to beckon me
 Nearer, my God, to thee,
  Nearer to thee!

4 Then, with my waking thoughts
 Bright with thy praise,
Out of my stony griefs
 Bethel I'll raise;
So by my woes to be
 Nearer, my God, to thee,
  Nearer to thee!

5 Or if, on joyful wing
 Cleaving the sky,
Sun, moon, and stars forgot,
 Upward I fly,
Still all my song shall be,
 Nearer, my God, to thee,
  Nearer to thee!

353   C. M.   M. E. H. 822.

Jesus! the name high over all,
  In hell, or earth, or sky;
Angels and men before it fall,
  And devils fear and fly.

2 Jesus! the name to sinners dear,
  The name to sinners given;
It scatters all their guilty fear;
  It turns their hell to heaven.

3 Jesus the prisoner's fetters breaks,
  And bruises Satan's head;
Power into strengthless souls he speaks,
  And life into the dead.

4 O that the world might taste and see
  The riches of his grace!
The arms of love that compass me
  Would all mankind embrace.

5 His only righteousness I show,
  His saving truth proclaim:
'Tis all my business here below,
  To cry, "Behold the Lamb!"

6 Happy, if with my latest breath
  I may but gasp his name;
Preach him to all, and cry in death,
  "Behold, behold the Lamb!"

354   7, 6.   M. E. H. 754.

I lay my sins on Jesus,
  The spotless Lamb of God;
He bears them all, and frees us
  from the accursèd load:
I bring my guilt to Jesus,
  To wash my crimson stains
White in his blood most precious,
  Till not a stain remains.

2 I lay my wants on Jesus,
  All fullness dwells in him;
He healeth my diseases,
  He doth my soul redeem:
I lay my griefs on Jesus,
  My burdens and my cares;
He from them all releases,
  He all my sorrows shares.

3 I rest my soul on Jesus,
  This weary soul of mine;
His right hand me embraces,
  I on his breast recline;
I love the name of Jesus,
  Immanuel, Christ, the Lord;
Like fragrance on the breezes,
  His name abroad is poured.

4 I long to be like Jesus,
  Meek, loving, lowly, mild;
I long to be like Jesus,
  The Father's holy child:
I long to be with Jesus
  Amid the heavenly throng,
To sing with saints his praises,
  And learn the angels' song.

355   C. P. M.   M. E. H. 743.

O could I speak the matchless worth,
O could I sound the glories forth,
  Which in my Saviour shine,
I'd soar and touch the heavenly strings,
And vie with Gabriel while he sings
  In notes almost divine.

2 I'd sing the precious blood he spilt,
My ransom from the dreadful guilt
  Of sin, and wrath divine;
I'd sing his glorious righteousness,
In which all-perfect, heavenly dress
  My soul shall ever shine.

3 I'd sing the characters he bears,
And all the forms of love he wears,
  Exalted on his throne;
In loftiest songs of sweetest praise,
I would to everlasting days
  Make all his glories known.

4 Well, the delightful day will come
When my dear Lord will bring me home,
  And I shall see his face;
Then with my Saviour, Brother, Friend,
A blest eternity I'll spend,
  Triumphant in his grace.

356   8, 7. d.   M. E. H. 726.

Come, thou Fount of every blessing,
  Tune my heart to sing thy grace;
Streams of mercy, never ceasing,
  Call for songs of loudest praise.
Teach me some melodious sonnet,
  Sung by flaming tongues above;
Praise the mount—I'm fixed upon it—
  Mount of thy redeeming love!

2 Here I'll raise mine Ebenezer;
  Hither by thy help I'm come;
And I hope, by thy good pleasure,
  Safely to arrive at home.
Jesus sought me when a stranger,
  Wandering from the fold of God;
He, to rescue me from danger,
  Interposed his precious blood.

3 O to grace how great a debtor
  Daily I'm constrained to be!
Let thy goodness, like a fetter,
  Bind my wandering heart to thee:
Prone to wander, Lord, I feel it,
  Prone to leave the God I love;
Here's my heart, O take and seal it;
  Seal it for thy courts above.

357 S. M. M. H. 797.

Blest be the tie that binds
  Our hearts in Christian love;
The fellowship of kindred minds
  Is like to that above.

2 Before our Father's throne,
  We pour our ardent prayers;
Our fears, our hopes, our aims are one,
  Our comforts and our cares.

3 We share our mutual woes,
  Our mutual burdens bear;
And often for each other flows
  The sympathizing tear.

4 When we asunder part,
  It gives us inward pain;
But we shall still be joined in heart,
  And hope to meet again.

5 This glorious hope revives
  Our courage by the way;
While each in expectation lives,
  And longs to see the day

6 From sorrow, toil, and pain,
  And sin we shall be free;
And perfect love and friendship reign
  Through all eternity.

358 8s. M. H. 747.

How tedious and tasteless the hours
  When Jesus no longer I see! [flowers,
Sweet prospects, sweet birds, and sweet
  Have all lost their sweetness to me;
The midsummer sun shines but dim,
  The fields strive in vain to look gay;
But when I am happy in him,
  December's as pleasant as May.

2 His name yields the richest perfume,
  And sweeter than music his voice;
His presence disperses my gloom,
  And makes all within me rejoice;
I should, were he always thus nigh,
  Have nothing to wish or to fear;
No mortal so happy as I,
  My summer would last all the year.

3 Content with beholding his face,
  My all to his pleasure resigned,
No changes of season or place
  Would make any change in my mind:
While blest with a sense of his love,
  A palace a toy would appear,
And prisons would palaces prove,
  If Jesus would dwell with me there.

4 My Lord, if indeed I am thine,
  If thou art my sun and my song,
Say, why do I languish and pine?
  And why are my winters so long?

O drive these dark clouds from my sky,
  Thy soul-cheering presence restore;
Or take me to thee up on high,
  Where winter and clouds are no more.

359 C. P. M. M. H. 657.

Come on, my partners in distress,
My comrades through the wilderness,
  Who still your bodies feel;
Awhile forget your griefs and fears,
And look beyond this vale of tears,
  To that celestial hill.

2 Beyond the bounds of time and space,
Look forward to that heavenly place,
  The saints' secure abode;
On faith's strong eagle pinions rise,
And force your passage to the skies,
  And scale the mount of God.

3 Who suffer with our Master here,
We shall before his face appear
  And by his side sit down;
To patient faith the prize is sure,
And all that to the end endure
  The cross, shall wear the crown.

4 Thrice blessed, bliss-inspiring hope!
It lifts the fainting spirits up,
  It brings to life the dead:
Our conflicts here shall soon be past,
And you and I ascend at last,
  Triumphant with our Head.

5 That great mysterious Deity
We soon with open face shall see;
  The beatific sight [praise,
Shall fill the heavenly courts with
And wide diffuse the golden blaze
  Of everlasting light.

360 L. M. M. H. 919.

Jesus shall reign where'er the sun
Does his successive journeys run;
His kingdom spread from shore to
  shore, [more.
Till moons shall wax and wane no

2 From north to south the princes meet,
To pay their homage at his feet;
While western empires own their Lord,
And savage tribes attend his word.

3 To him shall endless prayer be made,
And endless praises crown his head;
His name like sweet perfume shall rise
With every morning sacrifice.

4 People and realms of every tongue
Dwell on his love with sweetest song,
And infant voices shall proclaim
Their early blessings on his name.

361 7s. d. M. E. H. 935.

Watchman, tell us of the night,
  What its signs of promise are.
Traveler, o'er yon mountain's height
  See that glory-beaming star!
Watchman, does its beauteous ray
  Aught of hope or joy foretell?
Traveler, yes; it brings the day,
  Promised day of Israel.

2 Watchman, tell us of the night;
  Higher yet that star ascends.
Traveler, blessedness and light,
  Peace and truth, its course portends!
Watchman, will its beams alone
  Gild the spot that gave them birth?
Traveler, ages are its own,
  See, it bursts o'er all the earth!

3 Watchman, tell us of the night,
  For the morning seems to dawn.
Traveler, darkness takes its flight;
  Doubt and terror are withdrawn.
Watchman, let thy wandering cease;
  Hie thee to thy quiet home!
Traveler, lo! the Prince of Peace,
  Lo! the Son of God is come!

362 7, 6. M. E. H. 930.

From Greenland's icy mountains,
  From India's coral strand;
Where Afric's sunny fountains
  Roll down their golden sand;
From many an ancient river,
  From many a palmy plain,
They call us to deliver
  Their land from error's chain.

2 What though the spicy breezes
  Blow soft o'er Ceylon's isle;
Though every prospect pleases,
  And only man is vile?
In vain with lavish kindness
  The gifts of God are strewn;
The heathen in his blindness
  Bows down to wood and stone.

3 Shall we, whose souls are lighted
  With wisdom from on high,
Shall we to men benighted
  The lamp of life deny?
Salvation! O salvation!
  The joyful sound proclaim,
Till earth's remotest nation
  Has learned Messiah's name.

4 Waft, waft, ye winds, his story,
  And you, ye waters, roll,
Till, like a sea of glory,
  It spreads from pole to pole:
Till o'er our ransomed nature
  The Lamb for sinners slain,
Redeemer, King, Creator,
  In bliss returns to reign.

363 11, or 13, 11, 12. M. E. H. 998.

I would not live alway; I ask not to stay
  [the way
Where storm after storm rises dark o'er
The few lucid mornings that dawn on us here
  [for its cheer.
Are enough for life's woes, full enough

2 I would not live alway; no, welcome the tomb!
  [its gloom;
Since Jesus hath lain there. I dread not
There sweet be my rest till he bids me arise,
  [skies.
To hail him in triumph descending the

3 Who, who would live alway, away from his God;
  [bode,
Away from yon heaven, that blissful a-
Where the rivers of pleasure flow o'er the bright plains,
  [reigns?
And the noontide of glory eternally

4 Where the saints of all ages in harmony meet,
  [to greet;
Their Saviour and brethren transported
While the anthems of rapture unceasingly roll,
  [of the soul.
And the smile of the Lord is the feast

364 8, 7. d. M. E. H. 776.

Glorious things of thee are spoken,
  Zion, city of our God;
He, whose word cannot be broken,
  Formed thee for his own abode;
On the Rock of ages founded,
  What can shake thy sure repose?
With salvation's walls surrounded,
  Thou mayst smile at all thy foes.

2 See the streams of living waters,
  Springing from eternal love,
Still supply thy sons and daughters,
  And all fear of want remove;
Who can faint while such a river
  Ever flows our thirst to assuage?
Grace, which, like the Lord, the giver,
  Never fails from age to age.

3 Round each habitation hovering,
  See the cloud and fire appear,
For a glory and a covering,
  Showing that the Lord is near!
He who gives us daily manna,
  He who listens when we cry,
Let him hear the loud hosanna
  Rising to his throne on high.

365   C. M.   M. E. H. 945.

Come, let us use the grace divine,
And all, with one accord,
In a perpetual covenant join
  Ourselves to Christ the Lord ;
2 Give up ourselves, through Jesus'
  His name to glorify ;   [power,
And promise, in this sacred hour,
  For God to live and die.
3 The covenant we this moment make
  Be ever kept in mind ;
We will no more our God forsake,
  Or cast his words behind.
4 We never will throw off his fear
  Who hears our solemn vow ;
And if thou art well pleased to hear,
  Come, down, and meet us now.
5 Thee, Father, Son, and Holy Ghost,
  Let all our hearts receive ;
Present with the celestial host,
  The peaceful answer give.
6 To each the covenant blood apply,
  Which takes our sins away ;
And register our names on high,
  And keep us to that day.

366   11, 10.   M. E. H. 683.

Come, ye disconsolate, where'er ye languish ;   [kneel ;
Come to the mercy-seat, fervently
Here bring your wounded hearts, here tell your anguish ;   [not heal.
Earth has no sorrow that Heaven can-
2 Joy of the desolate, light of the straying,   [pure,
Hope of the penitent, fadeless and
Here speaks the Comforter, tenderly saying,   [not cure."
"Earth has no sorrow that Heaven can-
3 Here see the bread of life; see waters flowing   [from above ;
Forth from the throne of God, pure
Come to the feast of love ; come, ever knowing   [remove.
Earth has no sorrow but Heaven can

367   C. M.   M. E. H. 1037.

There is a land of pure delight,
  Where saints immortal reign ;
Infinite day excludes the night,
  And pleasures banish pain.
2 There everlasting spring abides,
  And never-withering flowers :
Death, like a narrow sea, divides
  This heavenly land from ours.

3 Sweet fields beyond the swelling flood
  Stand dressed in living green ;
So to the Jews old Canaan stood,
  While Jordan rolled between.
4 Could we but climb where Moses
  And view the landscape o'er, [stood,
Not Jordan's stream, nor death's cold
  Should frightus from the shore. [flood,

368   8, 6.   M. E. H. 1039.

There is an hour of peaceful rest,
  To mourning wanderers given ;
There is a joy for souls distressed,
  A balm for every wounded breast,
'Tis found above, in heaven.
2 There is a home for weary souls
  By sin and sorrow driven, [shoals,
When tossed on life's tempestuous
Where storms arise and ocean rolls,
  And all is drear ; 'tis heaven.
3 There faith lifts up the tearless eye,
  To brighter prospects given ;
And views the tempest passing by,
The evening shadows quickly fly,
  And all serene in heaven.
4 There fragrant flowers immortal bloom,
  And joys supreme are given ;
There rays divine disperse the gloom.
Beyond the confines of the tomb
  Appears the dawn of heaven.

369   7, 6.   M. E. H. 932.

The morning light is breaking ;
  The darkness disappears ;
The sons of earth are waking
  To penitential tears ;
Each breeze that sweeps the ocean
  Brings tidings from afar,
Of nations in commotion,
  Prepared for Zion's war.
2 See heathen nations bending
  Before the God we love,
And thousand hearts ascending
  In gratitude above ;
While sinners, now confessing,
  The gospel call obey,
And seek the Saviour's blessing,
  A nation in a day.
3 Blest river of salvation,
  Pursue thine onward way ;
Flow thou to every nation,
  Nor in thy riches stay :
Stay not till all the lowly
  Triumphant reach their home :
Stay not till all the holy
  Proclaim, "The Lord is come !"

370 L. M. M. E. H. 1072.

My heavenly home is bright and fair:
Nor pain nor death can enter there;
Its glittering towers the sun outshine;
That heavenly mansion shall be mine.

I'm going home, I'm going home,
I'm going home to die no more;
To die no more, to die no more,
I'm going home to die no more.

2 My Father's house is built on high,
Far, far above the starry sky,
When from this earthly prison free,
That heavenly mansion mine shall be.

3 While here, a stranger far from home,
Affliction's waves may round me foam;
Although, like Lazarus, sick and poor,
My heavenly mansion is secure.

4 Let others seek a home below,
Which flames devour, or waves o'erflow,
Be mine the happier lot to own
A heavenly mansion near the throne.

5 Then fail the earth, let stars decline,
And sun and moon refuse to shine,
All nature sink and cease to be,
That heavenly mansion stands for me.

371 7s. d. M. E. H. 936.

See how great a flame aspires,
  Kindled by a spark of grace!
Jesus' love the nations fires,
  Sets the kingdoms on a blaze.
To bring fire on earth he came;
  Kindled in some hearts it is:
O that all might catch the flame,
  All partake the glorious bliss!

2 When he first the work begun,
  Small and feeble was his day:
Now the word doth swiftly run;
  Now it wins its widening way:
More and more it spreads and grows,
  Ever mighty to prevail;
Sin's strongholds it now o'erthrows,
  Shakes the trembling gates of hell.

3 Sons of God, your Saviour praise!
  He the door hath opened wide;
He hath given the word of grace;
  Jesus' word is glorified.
Jesus, mighty to redeem,
  He alone the work hath wrought;
Worthy is the work of him, [naught.
  Him who spake a word from

4 Saw ye not the cloud arise,
  Little as a human hand?
Now it spreads along the skies,
  Hangs o'er all the thirsty land;
Lo! the promise of a shower
  Drops already from above;
But the Lord will shortly pour
  All the Spirit of his love.

372 C. M. M. E. H. 1030.

How happy every child of grace,
  Who knows his sins forgiven!
"This earth," he cries, "is not my
  I seek my place in heaven,— [place,
A country far from mortal sight;
  Yet O, by faith I see
The land of rest, the saints' delight,
  The heaven prepared for me."

2 O what a bless'd hope is ours!
  While here on earth we stay,
We more than taste the heavenly
  And antedate that day: [powers,
We feel the resurrection near,
  Our life in Christ concealed,
And with his glorious presence here
  Our earthen vessels filled.

3 O would he more of heaven bestow,
  And let the vessels break,
And let our ransomed spirits go
  To grasp the God we seek;
In rapturous awe on him to gaze,
  Who bought the sight for me;
And shout and wonder at his grace
  Through all eternity!

373 C. M. M. E. H. 1038.

On Jordan's stormy banks I stand,
  And cast a wishful eye
To Canaan's fair and happy land,
  Where my possessions lie.

2 O the transporting, rapturous scene,
  That rises to my sight!
Sweet fields arrayed in living green,
  And rivers of delight.

3 O'er all those wide-extended plains
  Shines one eternal day;
There God the Son forever reigns,
  And scatters night away.

4 No chilling winds, or poisonous breath,
  Can reach that healthful shore;
Sickness and sorrow, pain and death,
  Are felt and feared no more.

5 When shall I reach that happy place,
  And be forever blest?
When shall I see my Father's face,
  And in his bosom rest?

6 Filled with delight, my raptured soul
  Would here no longer stay:
Though Jordan's waves around me
  Fearless I'd launch away. [roll,

374   The Cross! the Cross!

The cross! the cross! the blood-stained
The hallowed cross I see !   [cross !
Reminding me of precious blood
That once was shed for me.

Cho.—Oh, the blood ! the prec'ous blood!
   That Jesus shed for me
Upon the cross, in crimson flood,
   Just now by faith I see.

2 The cross! the cross! the heavy cross,
   The Saviour bore for me,   [grief,
Which bowed him to the earth with
   On sad Mount Calvary.

4 How light! how light! this precious
   Presented to my view,   [cross,
And while, with care, I take it up,
   Behold the crown my due.

4 The crown! the crown! the glorious
   The crown of victory !   [crown !
The crown of life ! it shall be mine
   When Jesus I shall see.

5 My tears, unbidden, seem to flow
   For love, unbounded love,   [woe,
Which guides me through this world of
   And points to joys above.

375   Precious Promise.

Precious promise God hath given
   To the weary passer-by,
On the way from earth to heaven,
   "I will guide thee with mine eye."

Ref.—I will guide thee, I will guide thee,
   I will guide thee with mine eye;
On the way from earth to heaven,
   I will guide thee with mine eye.

2 When temptations almost win thee,
   And thy trusted watchers fly,
Let this promise ring within thee,
   "I will guide thee with mine eye."

3 When thy secret hopes have perished,
   In the grave of years gone by,
Let this promise still be cherished,
   "I will guide thee with mine eye."

4 When the shades of life are falling,
   And the hour has come to die,
Hear thy trusty Pilot calling,
   "I will guide thee with mine eye."

376   Parting Hymn.

Saviour, again to thy dear name we
   raise,   [praise ;
With one accord our parting hymn of
We stand to bless thee ere our worship
   cease,   [peace.
Then, lowly kneeling, wait thy word of

2 Grant us thy peace upon our heaven-
   ward way ;   [the day ;
With thee began, with thee shall end,
Guard thou the lips from sin, the hearts
   from shame,   [name.
That in this house have called upon thy

3 Grant us thy peace, Lord, through
   the coming night,
Turn thou for us its darkness into light;
From harm and danger keep thy chil-
   dren free,   [thee.
For dark and light are both alike to

4 Grant us thy peace throughout our
   earthly life,   [strife ;
Our balm in sorrow and our stay in
Then, when thy voice shall bid our con-
   flict cease,
Call us, O Lord, to thy eternal peace.

377   Sorrow is o'er.

What to me are earth's pleasures and
   what its flowing tears?
What are all the sorrows I deplore?
There's a song ever swelling—still lin-
   gers on my ears :
Oh, sorrow shall come again no more.

Cho.—'Tis a song from the home of the
   weary :
Sorrow, sorrow is forever o'er ;
Happy now, ever happy on Canaan's
   peaceful shore,
Oh, sorrow shall come again no more.

2 I seek not earthly glory, nor mingle
   with the gay,
I covet not this world's gilded store,
There are voices now calling from the
   bright realms of day,
Oh, sorrow shall come again no more.

3 Though here I'm sad and drooping,
   and weep my life away,   [shore,
With a lone heart still clinging to the
Yet I hear happy voices which ever
   seem to say,
Oh, sorrow shall come again no more.

4 'Tis a note that is wafted across the
   troubled wave,   [shore,
'Tis a song that I've heard upon the
'Tis a sweet thrilling murmur around
   the Christian's grave,
Oh, sorrow shall come again no more.

5 'Tis the loud-pealing anthem—the
   victor's holy song,   [o'er ;
Where the strife and the conflict are
When the saved ones forever, in joyous
   notes prolong,
Oh, sorrow shall come again no more.

378 Bringing in the Sheaves.

Sowing in the morning, sowing seeds
of kindness,   [eves;
Sowing in the noon-tide and the dewy
Waiting for the harvest, and the time
of reaping,   [the sheaves.
We shall come rejoicing, bringing in
Cho.—Bringing in the sheaves, bring-
ing in the sheaves, [the sheaves,
We shall come rejoicing, bringing in
Bringing in the sheaves, bringing in
the sheaves,   [the sheaves.
We shall come rejoicing, bringing in

2 Sowing in the sunshine, sowing in
the shadows,   [chilling breeze;
Fearing neither clouds nor winter's
By and by the harvest, and the labor
ended,   [the sheaves.
We shall come rejoicing, bringing in

3 Go, then, ever weeping, sowing for
the Master,   [often grieves;
Though the loss sustained our spirit
When our weeping's over, he will bid
us welcome,   [the sheaves.
We shall come rejoicing, bringing in

379 I know I love Thee better.

I know I love thee better, Lord,
Than any earthly joy,
For thou hast given me the peace
Which nothing can destroy.
Cho.—The half has never yet been told,
Of love so full and free;
The half has never yet been told,
The blood - it cleanseth me.

2 I know that thou art nearer still
Than any earthly throng,
And sweeter is the thought of thee
Than any lovely song.

3 Thou hast put gladness in my heart;
Then well may I be glad!
Without the secret of thy love
I could not but be sad.

4 O Saviour, precious Saviour mine!
What will thy presence be,
If such a life of joy can crown
Our walk on earth with thee?

380 Oh, Bliss of the Purified!

Oh, bliss of the purified! bliss of the
free!   [me!
I plunge in the crimson tide open for
O'er sin and uncleanness exulting I
stand,   [his hand.
And point to the print of the nails in

Cho.—Oh, sing of his mighty love,
Sing of his mighty love,
Sing of his mighty love—
Mighty to save!

2 Oh, bliss of the purified! Jesus is
mine,   [pine;
No longer in dread condemnation I
In conscious salvation I sing of his
grace,   [face!
Who lifted upon me the smiles of his

3 Oh, bliss of the purified! bliss of the
pure!   [cannot cure;
No wound hath the soul that his blood
No sorrow-bowed head but may sweet-
ly find rest,—   [breast.
No, tears but may dry them on Jesus'

4 O Jesus the Crucified! thee will I
sing!   [my King!
My blessed Redeemer! my God and
My soul, filled with rapture, shall shout
o'er the grave,   [TO SAVE.
And triumph at death, in the MIGHTY

381 On the Cross.

BEHOLD! behold! the Lamb of God,
On the cross, on the cross;
For you he shed his precious blood,
On the cross, on the cross.
Now hear his all-important cry,
"Eloi lama sabacthani;"
Draw near and see your Saviour die,
On the cross, on the cross.

2 Come, sinners see him lifted up,
On the cross, on the cross;
He drinks for you the bitter cup,
On the cross, on the cross.
To heaven he turns his languid eyes,
"'Tis finished," now the conqueror cries,
Then bows his sacred head and dies,
On the cross, on the cross.

3 'Tis done! the mighty deed is done,
On the cross, on the cross;
The battle fought, the victory won,
On the cross, on the cross.
The rocks do rend, the mountains quake,
While Jesus doth atonement make,
While Jesus suffers for your sake,
On the cross, on the cross.

4 Where'er I go I'll tell the story
Of the cross, of the cross;
In nothing else my soul shall glory
Save the cross, save the cross.
Yes, this my constant theme shall be,
Through time and in eternity,
That Jesus suffered death for me,
On the cross, on the cross.

382 My days are gliding.

My days are gliding swiftly by,
And I, a pilgrim stranger,
Would not detain them as they fly!
Those hours of toil and danger.
Cho.—For oh, we stand on Jordan's
Our friends are passing over, [strand,
And just before, the shining shore
We may almost discover.

2 We'll gird our loins, my brethren dear,
Our distant home discerning;
Our absent Lord has left us word,
Let every lamp be burning,—

3 Should coming days be cold and dark,
We need not cease our singing;
That perfect rest naught can molest,
Where golden harps are ringing.

4 Let sorrow's rudest tempests blow,
Each chord on earth to sever,
Our King says, come, and there's our
Forever, oh, forever! [home,

383 I am on my way to Zion.

O when shall I see Jesus, and dwell
with him above, [lasting love.
To drink the flowing fountain of ever-
Cho.—I am on my way to Zion,
To the new Jerusalem.

2 Through grace I am determined to
conquer though I die, [I'll fly.
And away to Jesus, on wings of love

3 And if you meet with trials and troubles on your way;
Cast all your care on Jesus, and don't forget to pray.

3 Gird on the heavenly armor of faith,
and hope, and love,
And when your race is ended you'll
reign with him above.

384 The Old Ship of Zion.

What ship is this that is passing by?
O glory, hallelujah !
It's the old ship of Zion,
Hallelujah !

2 O, who is her captain and what is his
name ?
'Tis the meek and lowly Jesus.

3 Is your ship well built, are her timbers all sound?
Why, she's built of gospel timber.

4 Do you think she will safely land her
crew ?
Why, she's landed thousands over,
And she'll land as many more.

385 L. M.

Happy day, happy day!
When Jesus washed my sins away,
He taught me how to watch and pray,
And live rejoicing every day.
Happy day, happy day!
When Jesus washed my sins away.

386 L. M.

Come to the Saviour, come,
O come to the Saviour, come,
His wounds for you stand open wide,
Come to the Saviour, come.

387 L. M.

Ho every one that thirsts!
Come ye to the waters,
Freely drink and quench your thirsts,
Zion's sons and daughters.

388 L. M.

We'll cross the river of Jordan,
Happy, happy,
We'll cross the river of Jordan,
Happy in the Lord.

389 L. M.

Save! O save, Save, mighty Lord,
And send converting power down !
Save, mighty Lord.

390 L. M.

O he's taken my feet from the mire and
the clay, [Ages.
And he's placed them on the Rock of

391 L. M.

[:Praise the Lord, praise the Lord, O
my soul.:]

392 L. M.

The cross, the cross, the precious cross,
The wondrous cross of Jesus:
From all our sin its guilt and power,
And every stain it frees us.
Then I'm clinging, clinging, clinging,
O I'm clinging to the cross,
Yes, I'm clinging, clinging, clinging,
Clinging to the cross.

393 C. M.

They'll sing their welcome home to me,
They'll sing their welcome home to me,
And the angels will stand on the
heavenly strand
And sing their welcome home,
Welcome home, welcome home,
And the angels will stand on the
heavenly strand
And sing their welcome home.

394 7, 6.
The cross of Christ I'll cherish,
  Its crucifixion bear;
All hail, reproach or sorrow,
  If Jesus lead me there.

395 8s.
In the sweet by and by,
We shall meet on that beautiful shore;
  In the sweet by and by,
We shall meet on that beautiful shore.

396 8, 7.
Rocks and storms I'll fear no more
When on that eternal shore;
Drop the anchor! Furl the sail!
I am safe with'n the veil!

397 C. M.
Help me, dear Saviour, thee to own,
  And ever faithful be,
And when thou sittest on thy throne,
  Dear Lord, remember me.

398 C. M.
Many are the friends who are waiting
  Happy on the golden strand, [to-day,
Many are the voices calling us away,
  To join their glorious band:
|: Calling us away, calling us away,
  Calling to the better land. :|

399 C. M.
Jesus died for you,
  Jesus died for me,
Yes, Jesus died for all mankind,
  Bless God, salvation's free.

400 C. M.
O for converting grace,
  And O for sanctifying power!
Lord, we beg for Jesus's sake,
  A sweet refreshing shower.

401 C. M.
There you'll sing hallelujah,
  And I'll sing hallelujah,
And we'll all sing hallelujah,
  In that bright world above.

402 C. M.
I now believe, I do believe,
  That Jesus died for me;
That on the cross he shed his blood,
  From sin to set me free.

403 C. M.
O Jesus! my Saviour, I look to thee,
  Remember, Lord, thy dying griefs,
  And then remember me.

404 C. M.
We will rest in the fair and happy land,
  Just across on the evergreen shore,
Sing the song of Moses and the Lamb
    by and by,
And dwell with Jesus evermore.

405 C. M.
Let us never mind the scoffs
  Nor the frowns of the world.
For we've all got the cross to bear;
  It will only make the crown
The brighter to shine,
  When we have the crown to wear.

406 C. M.
I want to go, I want to go,
  I want to go there too,
I want to go where Jesus is,
  I want to go there too.

407 S. M.
We're marching to Zion,
  Beautiful, beautiful Zion;
We're marching upward to Zion,
  The beautiful city of God.

408 S. M.
O, I'll be there, you'll be there,
Palms of victory, crowns of glory, we
    shall wear
In that beautiful world on high.

409 S. M.
I am coming, Lord,
  Coming now to thee,
Wash me, cleanse me in the blood
  That flowed on Calvary.

410 S. M.
|: I'm glad salvation's free, :|
Salvation's free for you and me,
  I'm glad salvation's free.

411 7s.
Let us walk in the light, walk in the light,
Walk in the light, in the light of God.

412 8, 7.
I will sprinkle you with water,
  I will cleanse you from all sin,
Sanctify and make you holy,
  I will come and dwell within.

413 7s.
|: Rock of Ages cleft for me, :|
  Let me hide myself in thee.

414 7s.
|: Oh redeemed, redeemed,
I'm washed in the blood of the Lamb. :|

DOXOLOGIES.

1   L. M.
Praise God, from whom all blessings flow;
Praise him, all creatures here below;
Praise him above, ye heavenly host;
Praise Father, Son, and Holy Ghost!

2   C. M.
To Father, Son, and Holy Ghost,
  The God whom we adore,
Be glory, as it was, is now,
  And shall be evermore!

3   C. M.
The God of mercy be adored,
  Who calls our souls from death,
Who saves by his redeeming word,
  And new-creating breath;
To praise the Father, and the Son,
  And Spirit all divine,—
The One in Three, and Three in One,—
  Let saints and angels join.

4   S. M.
To God, the Father, Son,
  And Spirit, One in Three,
Be glory, as it was, is now,
  And shall forever be.

5   L. M. 6l.
Immortal honor, endless fame,
Attend the almighty Father's name:
The Saviour Son be glorified,
Who for lost man's redemption died;
And equal adoration be,
Eternal Comforter, to thee!

6   H. M.
To God the Father's throne
  Your highest honors raise;
Glory to God the Son,
  To God the Spirit, praise:
With all our powers, eternal King,
Thy everlasting praise we sing.

7   7s.
Sing we to our God above,
Praise eternal as his love;
Praise him all ye heavenly host,
Father, Son, and Holy Ghost!

8   7, 6, 8.
Father, Son, and Holy Ghost,
  Thy Godhead we adore,
Join we with the heavenly host,
  To praise thee evermore!
Live, by earth and heaven adored,
  The Three in One, the One in Three,
Holy, holy, holy Lord,
  All glory be to thee!

9   C. P. M.
To Father, Son, and Holy Ghost,
The God whom heaven's triumphant host
And saints on earth adore;
Be glory as in ages past,
As now it is, and so shall last,
When time shall be no more!

10   7s. 6l.
Praise the name of God most high;
Praise him, all below the sky;
Praise him, all ye heavenly host,
Father, Son and Holy Ghost!
As through countless ages past,
Evermore his praise shall last.

11   8, 7, 4.
Great Jehovah! we adore thee,
  God the Father, God the Son,
God the Spirit, joined in glory
  On the same eternal throne:
    Endless praises
  To Jehovah, Three in One.

12   8, 7.
Praise the God of our salvation;
  Praise the Father's boundless love;
Praise the Lamb, our expiation;
  Praise the Spirit from above,
Author of the new creation,
  Him by whom our spirits live;
Undivided adoration
  To the one Jehovah give!

13   8s.
All praise to the Father, the Son,
  And Spirit, thrice holy and blest!
The eternal, supreme Three in One,
  Was, is, and shall still be confessed.

14   6, 4.
To God, the Father, Son,
And Spirit, Three in One,
  All praise be given!
Crown him, in every song;
To him your hearts belong:
Let all his praise prolong,
  On earth, in heaven!

15   7, 6.
To thee be praise forever,
  Thou glorious King of kings!
Thy wondrous love and favor
  Each ransomed spirit sings:
We'll celebrate thy glory,
  With all thy saints above,
And shout the joyful story
  Of thy redeeming love.

INDEX.

First Lines in roman; Titles in capitals.

	HYMN		HYMN		HYMN
Abide with me, fast falls	211	CHURCH RALLYING	96	Give to the winds thy	338
ABIDING,	5	CLEANSING WAVE,	222	GLORIA PATRI!	224
ABIDING IN HIM,	149	CLINGING AND RESTING	87	GLORIOUS FOUNTAIN,	147
Abiding, oh, so wondrous	149	Come, every soul by sin	204	Glorious things of thee	364
A charge to keep I have,	317	Come, Holy Spirit, heav-	273	Glory be to the Father,	223
A CHILD OF THE KING,	21	Come, humble sinner, in	280	GLORY TO GOD, HALLE-	23
Ah, my heart is heavy-la-	115	Come, let us join our	232	GLORY TO HIS NAME,	27
Ah, whither should I go,	286	Come, let us tune our	243	God be with you till we	95
Alas! alas! a wayward	176	Come, let us use the grace	365	God calling yet! shall I	288
Alas! and did my Saviour	262	Come, oh, come with me,	37	God came knocking,	126
ALEXANDRIA, C. M.,	145	Come on, my partners in	359	God is our refuge and	250
A little talk with Jesus,	6	Come, O thou Traveler	342	GOD KNOWS,	188
A little while together,	90	COME, PRODIGAL, COME	175	God loved the world so	56
ALL TO THEE,	160	COME, SINNER, COME,	206	God moves in a myster-	252
ALL THE WAY LONG IT	139	Come, sinners, to the gos-	283	GOD SO LOVED THE	56
All ye who pass by,	81	Come, the Saviour's call-	71	Go forth, O Christian sol-	142
Amazing grace! how	297	Come, thou almighty	231	Gracious Spirit, love di-	266
Am I a soldier of the	309	Come, thou fount of ev-	356	Great God, attend, while	247
And can it be that I	295	Come to the Saviour,	386	Guide me, O thou great	251
And can I yet delay,	291	Come unto me when sha-	322		
ANGELS' SONG,	152	Come, weary sinners,	281	Hail, hail, hail, beautiful	93
ARE YOU WASHED IN	175	Come, ye that 1. the Lord	240	Hail, thou once despised	260
Are you weary, are you	28	Come, ye that 1. the Sav.	238	Happy day! happy day!	385
Arise, my soul, arise,	306	Come, ye disconsolate,	366	Hark, hark, my soul!	152
A SINNER LIKE ME,	59	Come, ye sinners, poor	304	Hark, the glad sound!	256
As we journey by the	118	COMING TO-DAY,	174	Hasten, sinner, to be	279
A trembling soul I come	29	COMPANIONSHIP WITH.	48	Have mercy, Lord, on	151
AT THE CROSS,	98	CROSS OF CALVARY,	69	Have you been to Jesus	175
Author of faith, to thee I	293	CROWN HIM,	11	Have you not a word for	153
Awake, my soul, stretch	318			HEALING FOR THEE,	64
Awake! awake! our fes-	97	DEAR SAVIOUR, CLEANSE	29	HEAR MY CALL,	116
Awake! awake! the Mas-	96	Delay not, delay not, O.	285	He dies! the Friend of	265
		Depth of mercy, can	221	HE IS CALLING,	218
BACK TO THE FOLD,	168	Down at the cross where	27	He leadeth me! O bless-	335
BEAR ALOFT THE STAN-	51	Do you know how many	188	HE LOVES THEE STILL,	25
Beautiful light, holy and	172	Drooping souls, no lon-	220	HELP JUST A LITTLE,	103
Beautiful valley of Eden	192			Help me, dear Saviour,	397
Behold! behold! the	381	Each cooing dove and	75	HE SAVES,	12
Behold the Ark of God,	150	ECCE HOMO,	81	Ho, every one that thirst	387
BEHOLD THE FIELDS	114	ENOUGH FOR ME,	45	HOLD THE LIGHT UP	44
Be it my only wisdom,	319	Eternity! where?	187	Holy, holy, holy, Lord	246
BEULAH LAND,	179	EVEN ME,	121	HOLY SPIRIT, COME,	165
Beyond the smiling and	227	EVERY DAY,	100	HOME OF THE SOUL,	79
Blessed Saviour, my Re-	184	Every day my soul is	4	HOMEWARD BOUND,	195
Blessed Saviour, my sal-	105			HOPE'S BRIGHT STAR,	93
Blest be the tie that binds	357	Fade, fade, each earthly.	205	HOPEFULLY TRUSTING,	20
Blow ye the trumpet,	282	FAREWELL TO SORROW	33	Hover o'er me, Holy	171
Brother for Christ's king-	103	Father, I stretch my	296	How do thy mercies	255
BY THE GRACE OF GOD	58	FILL ME NOW,	171	How firm a foundation,	327
		FOLLOW THE LAMB,	157	How gentle God's com-	245
Called to the feast by	158	Forever here my rest shall	314	How happy every child	372
CALVARY,	70	Forever with the Lord,	123	How sweet the name of	274
Children of the heavenly	345	From all that dwell be-	241	How tedious and tasteless	358
Children of the kingdom	53	From every stormy wind	89		
CHRIST FOR ME,	124	From Greenland's icy	362	I am coming, Lord,	409
CHRIST IS ALL,	74	FROM THIS HOUR,	167	I am coming to the cross	212
CHRIST SHALL REIGN,	92			I am dwelling on the	31
CHRIST THE LORD IS	128	Gently, Lord, O gently	336	I am saved! the Lord	84

253

I am thinking of home of	195	Jesus, a word, a look, . 267	Lord, we are vile, con- . 277
I bring my sins to thee,	47	Jesus bids you come, . 214	Lord, we come before . 234
I dare not idle stand .	127	Jesus died for me, . . 399	Lord, when we bend be- 237
I do repent of every sin,	69	Jesus, here I bring my all	160	Love divine, all love ex- 302
I entered once a home .	74	Jesus, I come to thee, . 101	
If I in thy likeness, O .	119	JESUS IS CALLING YOU . 154	Many are the friends . 398
If, on a quiet sea, . .	333	JESUS IS MINE, . . 205	Many souls on life's dark 44
I have a crown, a kingly	33	Jesus I will trust thee, . 38	MARCHING ONWARD, . 26
I have a garden fair, .	24	Jesus my advocate above 258	May I draw nigh with . 25
I have entered the val-.	129	Jesus, my all, to heaven . 301	MEET ME THERE, . . 130
I have found a friend in	66	Jesus, my Lord, to thee, 132	MEMORIES OF GALLI- . 75
I have found the dearest	164	Jesus, my Lord, to thee I 9	MERCY SEAT, . . 89
I have given my all to .	108	JESUS, MY SAVIOUR AND 164	'Mid scenes of confusion 133
I have laid my burden .	39	JESUS OF NAZARETH . 161	MIGHTY JESUS SAVES, . 82
I heard thy voice calling	168	JESUS PAID IT ALL, . 199	MIGHTY TO SAVE, . . 91
I hear the Saviour say, .	199	JESUS SAVES, . . 85	More love to thee, O . 348
I hope to meet you all .	80	JESUS SAVES ME NOW, . 107	Must Jesus bear the cross 305
I know I love thee bet-	379	Jesus, Saviour, Lord of . 163	My days are gliding swift- 382
I know that my Redeem-	259	Jesus shall reign where'er 360	My faith looks up to thee 343
I lay my sins on Jesus, .	354	Jesus speaks in accents . 41	My Father is rich in . 208
I'LL LIVE FOR HIM, .	155	Jesus! the name high over 353	My God, how wonderful 253
I love thy kingdom Lord	349	Jesus the Saviour is pass- 64	My God, my Life, my . 346
I love to tell the story, .	120	Jesus, the very thought of 332	My God, the spring of . 337
I'm glad salvation's free,	410	Jesus, thine all-victorious 313	My gracious Lord, I own 324
I'M HOLDING ON, . .	73	Jesus, thou all-redeeming 235	My heart is fixed, eternal 124
I'M KNEELING AT THE .	57	Jesus, thou everlasting . 230	My heavenly home is . 370
I'm more than conqueror	162	Jesus, thy blood and . 270	My hope is built on noth- 209
I NEED THEE, . .	184	Jesus, where'er thy peo- 233	My Jesus, as thou wilt, . 334
I now believe, I do be-.	402	JESUS WILL GIVE YOU . 13	My life, my love I give . 155
In some way or other .	216	JESUS, WITH THEE, . 132	My soul, be on thy guard, 182
IN THE BOOK OF LIFE, .	34	JOY COMETH IN THE . 99	My soul for light and . 5
In the Christian's home .	213	Joy! joy! joy! wonder- . 92	My way is dreary and . 200
In the cross of Christ I .	263	Joy to the world! the . 248	
In the darkest hour, .	201	Just as I am, without one 9	Nearer, my God, to thee, 352
IN THE MORNING, . .	16	JUST FOR TO-DAY, . . 109	Never further than thy . 264
In the secret of his pres-	122		NOT MY LOVE, . . 163
In the silent midnight .	289	Keeep looking unto Je- 15	
In the sweet by and by,	395	Keep your colors flying, 86	O come and dwell in me 290
In thy book, where glory	34	KNEELING, PLEADING, . 151	O could I speak the . 355
In thy name, O Lord, .	236		Of him who did salvation 278
INVOCATION, . . .	225	Lamb of God whose dy- 55	O for a faith that will not 312
I praise the Lord that .	207	Lead, kindly light, amid 330	O for a glance of heaven- 287
I SHALL BE SATISFIED, .	119	LET HIM IN, . . . 72	O for a heart to praise my 315
I SHALL HAVE WINGS, .	196	Let us never mind the . 405	O for a thousand 156, 228
IS MY NAME WRITTEN .	32	Let us walk in the light, 411	O for converting grace, . 400
IS NOT THIS THE LAND	31	LIFE EVERLASTING, . 60	O God, thy power is won- 249
I stand all bewildered, .	20	LIFT UP YOUR HEADS, . 54	O good old way, how . 139
Is there any one here .	112	Light after darkness, . 43	O glorious hope of per- 325
I thirst, thou wounded .	307	Light in our darkness, . 117	O happy day, that fixed . 298
IT IS GOOD TO BE HERE	194	Light of all who come to 116	O happy day! what a . 52
IT IS WELL WITH MY .	50	Living for the Master, . 94	Oh, blessed fellowship . 48
It may not be our lot to	323	Look above, oh, look a- 159	Oh, bliss of the purified! 380
I've nothing to bring to .	110	LOOK AND LIVE, . . 113	O he's taken my feet, . 390
I've reached the land of	179	Looking unto Jesus, . 104	Oh, how happy are they, 194
I want to be a worker .	140	Look to the cross, sinner, 113	Oh, now I see the cleans- 222
I want to go, I want to .	406	Look up! behold the . 114	O holy Saviour! Friend 226
I was once far away from	59	Look, ye saints, the sight 11	Oh, redeemed, redeemed 414
I will look to the hills, .	186	Lord, for to-morrow and 109	Oh, sing to me of heaven 210
I will sing you a song, .	79	Lord, how secure and . 294	Oh, sometimes the shad- 8
I will sprinkle you with .	412	Lord, I am thine, entirely 10	Oh, the song of the soul 178
I WILL TRUST IN THEE,	105	Lord, I believe a rest re- 299	OH! 'TIS GLORY IN MY . 135
I would be thine, . .	145	Lord, I care not for . 32	Oh, weary pilgrim, lift . 99
I would not live alway;	363	Lord, I hear of showers 121	Oh, ye who would jour- 62

INDEX.

Title	Page	Title	Page	Title	Page
O I'll be there, you'll be	408	Rocks and storms I'll	396	There's a voice that comes	196
O it is hard to work for	321			There's a wideness in	218
O Jesus, immaculate	157	Saved by his goodness I	21	There's a wonderful story	78
O Jesus, Lord, thy dy-	98	Save, O save, save, mighty	389	There you'll sing hallelu-	401
O Jesus my Saviour, I	403	Saviour, again to thy dear	376	THE ROCK THAT IS	8
O Lord, thy work revive,	347	Saw ye my Saviour,	197	THE ROYAL COMMAND,	41
O love divine, how sweet	316	See how great a flame as-	371	THE SINNER'S INVITA-	215
O love surpassing know-	45	Shall we meet beyond the	143	THE SOLID ROCK,	209
On Calvary's brow my	70	Shout for joy, ye holy	128	THE SONG OF THE SOUL	178
One by one, our loved	67	Show pity, Lord, O Lord,	292	THE SUNSET OF THE	144
One more day its twilight	193	Sing glory to God in the	12	THE TONGUE OF PRAISE	156
On Jordan's stormy banks	373	Sing, my soul! proclaim	61	THE VALLEY OF BLESS-	129
On let us go where the	83	Sing on, ye joyful pilgrim	180	They'll sing their wel-	393
Only a beam of sunshine	134	Sinner, go, will you go,	215	This God is the God we	257
ONLY ONE WAY,	62	SONGS IN THE CALM,	131	This is the glorious gos-	107
ONLY REMEMBERED,	40	Sound a living war cry,,	51	Though my sins were	169
ONLY TRUST HIM,	204	Sound, sound the jubilee	18	Though there may be	100
On the happy, golden	130	Sound the battle-cry,	22	Though troubles assail	30
Onward now! the trum-	198	Sowing in the morning,	378	Though weak my faith,	73
Open the heavens and	225	Stand at your post, ye	136	Thou God of power,	229
Open the windows of the	35	Stand up! stand up for	183	THOU WILT DEFEND US,	117
O that my load of sin	311	Stay, thou insulted Spirit,	284	Through the gates of	58
O the bitter shame and	217	Sun of my soul, thou Sav-	244	Thy presence gracious	239
O think of a home over	102	SWEET HOME,	133	Thy way, not mine, O	328
O thou God of my salva-	351	Sweet hour of prayer,	326	'Tis the Lord who lead-.	131
O thou who driest the	335	Sweet is the work, my God	242	To the cross I long was.	87
O turn ye, O turn ye, for	269	Sweet land of rest, for	203	To the cross of Christ, my	14
OUR GLAD JUBILEE,	1			TO THE RESCUE,	118
Our sins on Christ were	268	TAKE ME AS I AM,	9	To thy cross, dear Christ,	135
Out on the desert, look-.	174	Talk with us, Lord, thy-	344	Touch my spirit with	106
Out on an ocean all	195	TELL IT TO JESUS,	28	TREASURES OF HEAVEN	49
OUTSIDE THE FOLD,	200	THAT OLD, OLD, STORY	78	TRUE AND FAITHFUL,	4
OUTSIDE THE GATE,	17	THE ALTERED MOTTO,	217	Trusting in Jesus there's	60
OVERCOMERS,	138	THE ARK FLOATETH BY	150	Trustingly, trustingly,	177
OVER THERE,	102	THE BEAUTIFUL HILLS,	186	TRUSTING ONLY THEE,	38
O what amazing words	275	The blood, the blood, is	57	TRUST IN THY DELIV-	142
O what shall I do my Sav-	300	THE CHILD OF A KING,	208	Trust on! trust on! be-	148
O when shall I see Jesus,	383	The cross and the Bible,	166	Try us, O God, and search	350
O who is this that com-.	91	The cross of Christ I'll	394		
		The cross! the cross!	374, 392	UNTIL YE FIND,	176
Peace, troubled soul, thou	254	The fountain of salvation	125	UNTO HIM THAT HATH	108
Peter on the troubled sea,	82	The God of Abra'hm	63	Unto us a Child is born,	88
PLEADING WITH THEE,	190	THE GOLDEN KEY,	219	Up and away, like the	40
Poor, starving soul, there's	17	The great Physician now	182		
Praise the Lord, praise	391	The home-land! oh, the.	65	Vain, delusive world,	303
Praise ye the Lord, the	141	THE LILY OF THE VAL-	66		
Prayer is the key,	219	THE LORD WILL PRO-	216	Wake, wake the song!	1
Prayer is the soul's sin-	341	The Master is come,	36	WALKING IN THE	94
PRECIOUS BIBLE,	24	THE MASTER'S CALL,	36	Walk in the light! so	46
Precious Jesus, Saviour	165	The morning light is	369	WASHED WHITE AS	169
Precious promise, God	375	THE NEW SONG,	170	Watchman, tell us of the	361
		THE NUMBERLESS HOST,	10	We are marching, march-	26
Redeemed, how I love to	7	THE PRODIGAL,	68	WE ARE MORE THAN	42
REDEEMED, PRAISE THE	52	There are lonely hearts	173	We are never, never wea-	23
REFUGE,	201	There are songs of joy	170	We are pilgrims looking	16
REJOICING EVERMORE,	30	There is a fountain filled	147	We are praying, blessed	167
Rejoice, the Lord is King	271	There is a land of pure	367	Weary and thirsty, oh,	190
REMEMBER CALVARY,	55	There is an eye that never	340	We have heard a joyful	85
REST,	106	There is an hour of peace	368	We'll cross the river of	388
REST FOR THE WEARY,	213	THERE'S A BLESSING AT	39	We're marching to Zion,	407
RESTING AT THE CROSS,	14	There's a crown in hea-.	49	WE SHALL KNOW,	76
Resting on the faithful-	189	There's an undertone of	144	We will rest in the fair	404
Rock of ages, cleft	276, 413	There's a stranger at the	72	What a Friend we have	185

255

What means this eager, . 161	When the mists have . 76	Why do you wait a con-. 154
What shall separate us, . 42	WHEN THE SHEAVES . 146	Why stand I here amid . 68
What ship is this that is . 384	When we enter the por-. 10	Will you come, with your 13
What to me are earth's . 377	While Jesus whispers to . 206	With joy we meditate the 272
When I can read my title 329	WHILE THE DAYS ARE 173	Work, for the night is . 320
When I survey the won- 261	While we bow in thy . 194	
When peace, like a river, 50	Who is this that cometh, . 54	Ye ransomed sinners, hear 308
WHEN THE KING COMES 158	WHOSOEVER, . . 207	Yield not to temptation, . 183
When the laborers have 146	Who, who is he? . . 138	Zion stands with hills sur- 339

www.ingramcontent.com/pod-product-compliance
Lightning Source LLC
Chambersburg PA
CBHW032108220426
43664CB00008B/1179